KV-436-525

The European Monetary System

Origins, operation and outlook

by Jacques van YPERSELE
with the collaboration of Jean-Claude KOEUNE

Preface by Robert TRIFFIN

WOODHEAD-FAULKNER
CAMBRIDGE · ENGLAND

First published in 1985 for the Commission of the European Communities by the Office for Official Publications of the European Communities, Luxembourg
This edition published in 1985 by Woodhead-Faulkner Ltd
Fitzwilliam House, 32 Trumpington Street, Cambridge CB2 1QY, England

© ECSC-EEC-EAEC, Brussels · Luxembourg, 1984

Conditions of sale
All rights reserved. No part of this publication may be reproduced, stored in a retrieval system or transmitted in any form or by any means, electronic, mechanical, photocopying, recording or otherwise, without the prior permission of the copyright owner.

British Library Cataloguing in Publication Data
Ypersele, Jacques van
    The European monetary system: origins, operation and outlook.
    1. Money—European Economic Community countries
    I. Title   II. Koeune, Jean-Claude
    332.4'566'094   HG930.5

    ISBN 0-85941-313-6

Printed in Great Britain by St Edmundsbury Press, Bury St Edmunds, Suffolk

Preface

I am delighted to have been asked to write a foreword to a book which is destined to become required reading for years to come, not only for the expert, but also for the educated layman seeking to grasp the development of the *European Monetary System* (EMS) within the broader framework of the *World Monetary System* (WMS)—or should I say *Scandal*?

What Jacques van Ypersele de Strihou, whom I am privileged to count as a long-standing friend, and Jean-Claude Koeune set out to do is to explain in clear and simple terms the main political and economic motivations leading up to the negotiation of the EMS— forces which will, ultimately, dictate the success or failure of the negotiations for the final achievement of the full *economic and monetary*—and hence political—*union* of the Community.

Jacques van Ypersele speaks here with all the authority of a man who was himself one of the principal architects of the famous compromises 'à la belge' which were instrumental in bringing a particularly difficult negotiation to a successful conclusion. He has also been one of the most constructive figures in the management of the EMS, making positive contributions to the never-ending international quest for a means of reforming the world monetary system of which the EMS is a part. As Principal Private Adviser of the Belgian Finance Minister, and subsequently as head of the Belgian Prime Minister's economic staff, he was also responsible for bringing in unpopular, but unavoidably necessary, policies designed to cure his country of the ills caused by inflation and galloping deficits in its budget and balance of payments.

His view of the situation and his proposals for the way ahead seem to me eminently correct, and I can see nothing to add to them, except perhaps a few observations of my own, in which I shall try to avoid any fruitless re-hashing of the central issues already summarized so admirably by him.

1. 'Let sleeping dogs lie'

This old proverb, it seems to me, accurately sums up the reasons for all the foot-dragging which has for years delayed the adoption of the most glaring and pressing *concrete reforms which could be implemented without delay*.

In my opinion, the most crucial—and 'seminal'— of those reforms would be the creation of a *European Reserve Fund,* more indispensable than ever today to enable the Community to confront the threats of recurrent foreign exchange and banking crises weighing down on an international banking and monetary system (?) dominated by the role of 'parallel world currency' conferred on an inconvertible and wildly fluctuating paper-dollar.

The idea was first floated almost fifteen years ago, in December 1969, by the West German Chancellor Willy Brandt [1] at the first 'Summit Conference' of Heads of State and Government at the Hague. It was promptly submerged in a more ambitious, but temporizing—not to say 'stalling'—resolution calling for the gradual achievement of full *Economic and Monetary Union,* over a period of ten years.

The European Council meeting at Bremen (6 and 7 July 1978) and later at Brussels (4 and 5 December 1978) reiterated the determination of the Heads of State and Government to continue the process of achieving European Union in stages. A *European Monetary Fund,* 'implying the full and unrestricted utilization of the ECU as a reserve asset and means of settlement' was to be set up no later than 1 January 1981, but later postponed by the Luxembourg European Council (December 1980) to an 'appropriate time'. Despite the crying need for such a Fund, that 'appropriate time' is not yet in sight.

This continued procrastination can no doubt be partly put down to the ingrained resistance of all bureaucracies—including those of central banks—to change the routines to which they are accustomed. It is far easier to carry on with the same old habit of latching on to an existing currency—yesterday sterling, today the US dollar (despite its inconvertibility)—rather than the ECU, whose 'full and unrestricted utilization' continues to raise multiple objections.

Such objections are comprehensible with regard to the final stage of *Economic and Monetary Union,* which will demand at least the irrevocable stability of *nominal* exchange rates between Community currencies, if not the complete phasing out of national currencies and their replacement by the ECU. Those countries which, having achieved the greatest measure of success in bringing their inflation rates under control expect to remain creditors of their partners, refuse to become the 'milch cows' of those whose political leaders seem incapable of forcing their public opinion to accept the austerity policies indispensable to avoid excessive balance of payments deficits.

But progress towards the intermediate stage of the EMF (*European Monetary Fund,* which I would prefer to call *European Federal Bank*), in no way implies such financing. It recognizes that realignments in *nominal* exchange rates are desirable, as well as unavoidable in practice to stabilize, or restore rapidly, *real* exchange rates to competitive levels. [2]

The experience of the first five years of functioning of the EMS has proved the benefits of such a scheme to even the most sceptical observers. Fundamental equilibrium has been

---

[1] At the instance of Jean Monnet's Action Committee for the United States of Europe.

[2] This does not mean the total elimination of all surpluses or deficits on current account, but keeping them within a ceiling corresponding to those capital movements which are economically and humanely possible and desirable between the richer, more developed countries and the less wealthy, less-developed ones.

4

preserved by seven realignments in the central rates, [3] which have also brought compulsory FECOM financing down to extremely modest levels which have, in most cases, been repaid within a relatively short period of time. FECOM funding has rarely exceeded 2 000 million ECUs, accounted in April 1984 for no more than 2.5 % of total issues of ECUs, and has been totally amortized since then.

The floating exchange rates of the other currencies, in contrast, led to a pattern of successive under- and overvaluations of the US dollar, and to the lasting concentration of most, or all, FECOM investments in a non-member country: the United States.

As the authors of this book stress, a substantial strengthening of the FECOM has now become a matter of pressing urgency if Europe is to survive the exchange shocks likely to buffet Community currencies as a result of the long-awaited and hoped-for (by the United States as much as the rest of the world) fall of the dollar from its present grossly overvalued levels. But the concrete shape of that strengthening is still a matter for negotiation. And there, the negotiators will have to overcome the legitimate fears of the 'strong currency' nations—and of the central banks generally—as to the dangers of inflation and inconvertibility which the increased utilization of the ECU in a reformed EMS might entail.

These fears have already been to some extent allayed by three recent developments: a slowdown in the *overall* rate of inflation [4] and the degrees of *divergence* [5] between the national inflation rates of Community countries in recent years; and the considerable improvement in *balance of payments on current account* [6] in all Community Member States without exception. If this trend continues, it should enable both the frequency and amplitude of currency realignments to be reduced. Indeed, no realignment has proved necessary since March 1983.

But there is no guarantee that this trend will continue over the months and years ahead. The improvement in national balances of payments can be largely explained by the chronic deepening US deficit, which cannot be sustained on a long-term basis. And the unpopularity of today's anti-inflationary policies might well incline, or force, the governments of certain countries to reverse them tomorrow. If the Community is to be able to negotiate a significant strengthening of the EMS and the role of the ECU, therefore, it will first have to satisfy two distinct, but perfectly compatible, preconditions.

---

[3] As Henry C. Wallich, Member of the Board of Governors of the Federal Reserve System of the United States, has repeatedly stressed in numerous speeches, lectures and articles.

[4] The average annual rise in consumer prices for the Community as a whole has fallen by almost two-thirds since 1980, when it stood at 14.7 %, to 6.4 % between May 1983 and May 1984.

[5] Maximum differentials between all but three countries (Greece, Ireland and Italy) fell from more than 12 % in 1980 (5.4 % in the Federal Republic of Germany and 18 % in the United Kingdom) to 5 % between May 1983 and May 1984 (2.8 % in FR of Germany and 7.8 % in France).

[6] *Net deficits* of USD 13 000 million on the Community's current account in 1981 had turned into a USD 3 000 million *surplus* by 1983. OECD forecasts predict a USD 16 000 million surplus by 1985. All except two countries were running deficits totalling nearly USD 29 000 million in 1981. By 1983, these global deficits—leaving aside the surpluses of all other countries—totalled only USD 8 000 million: USD 4 000 million for France; USD 500 million for the Belgo-Luxembourg Union and USD 3 500 million for Denmark, Greece and Ireland together.

2. Agreement of principle over national readjustment policies

The first of these prerequisites is an *agreement of principle* between the governments presently in power expressing their determination to do their utmost to pursue those national policies essential to maintaining their balances of payments in fundamental equilibrium. This will probably still require occasional realignments in the central rates of national currencies *vis-à-vis* the ECU, but it should exclude the possibility of any depreciation of the ECU itself: indeed, the ECU is called upon to appreciate in terms of a grossly overvalued US dollar. Any further rise in already astronomical interest rates would also be ruled out; that would leave the necessary macro-economic readjustments to be looked for principally in the correction of budgetary deficits, which are clearly excessive in most Community countries as they are in the United States. [7]

3. Placing a ceiling on ECU issues

The second requirement is a reaffirmation of the fact that occasional policy failures will not be financed in the future—any more than they have been up to now—by excessive issues of ECUs, entailing for creditor countries the dual risk of increasing inflationary pressures at home and the loss of convertibility of their ECU holdings into foreign currencies—which for all practical purposes means the dollar—needed to finance their deficits with non-Community countries.

The issues of ECUs should be adjusted to financing the potential for non-inflationary growth of trade and production within the Community; their annual growth rate should be kept within a *presumptive ceiling* of x%, not to be exceeded except with the backing of a qualified majority vote of two-thirds or even more, and then only in situations of 'force majeure' such as the two explosions of oil price in recent years.

The *global* definition of such a ceiling would force *operationally* the authorities to make a clear-cut choice between financing credits to Member States and investing outside the Community—in dollars only for the time being, but perhaps in other approved currencies

---

[7] Two further points deserve consideration here:
  (a) The reduction of the present record levels of unemployment imposes the adoption by Europe of policies which have proved their effectiveness in the United States:
    — the moderation of nominal wage increases, whose indexation *de jure* or *de facto* should exclude the incidence of rises in the cost of imports and taxes necessary to balance the budgets;
    — greater flexibility in the excessively rigid minimum wages;
    — increased geographical and occupational mobility for workers, etc., etc.
  (b) In all the more opulent countries—in Europe as in the United States—three factors should stimulate governments into entering into international agreements which would enable them to apply future productivity gains to concerted reductions in working time rather than to increases in nominal stimulating consumer spending:
    — absorption of unemployment by an improved distribution of job opportunities;
    — the fight against inflation;
    — the need to devote a higher portion of the limited material resources of our planet to the essential investment and consumption increases in the Third World.

at a later date—which are the two counterparts of ECU issues. This would be both economically desirable and politically feasible. Any balance of payments surpluses which increase issues of ECUs in exchange for deposits in dollars or other currencies should normally reduce the borrowing needs of Member States; while, on the contrary those needs would increase—and be more difficult to combat politically—when external deficits lead to a reduction in the supply of ECUs issued against foreign exchange.

This non-inflationary ceiling on ECU issues must clearly exclude entirely what has thus far been the principal source (over 91 %) of the doubling of such issues over the five years since the inception of the EMS, and of their haphazard fluctuations up and down: ECUs issued against gold deposits have oscillated wildly with contractual rates for gold (close to market rates), rising from 14 000 million at the outset (164.9 ECU per ounce) to a maximum approaching 41 000 million at the end of 1983 (476.8 ECU per ounce), not falling to below 39 000 million by April 1984 (451.6 ECU per ounce). The authors highlight this absurdity on page 100, but make only a brief and enigmatic reference (p. 102) as to how it could be avoided in the future.

The most straightforward and palatable solution would probably be to exclude gold from the compulsory deposit system altogether, with a concomitant increase in deposits of dollars (and other approved currencies?), whose management by the Community is central to a concerted policy of intervention on the market. But this is neither the time nor the place to expound on the details of such a proposal, or of the various alternative proposals which I have myself put before the Commission's experts in the past, or of those mentioned in the Commission's own publications. [8]

In the long run, and as part of a complete overhaul of the *world* monetary system,—the FECOM or its eventual successor, the *European Federal Bank*—should no longer hold international reserves in gold or national currencies, but only in international monetary reserve accounts with the *International Monetary Fund*.

In the meantime, the book-keeping profits and losses recorded by central banks on their international reserves should be frozen in 'escrow' accounts. Account-holder countries would only be entitled to draw on them as an alternative to, and on the same terms as, loans from the FECOM, or to repay FECOM loans. Admittedly, central banks do, on the whole, seek to defer as long as possible the increased opportunities for inflation presented to governments by the book-keeping profits made by recording at the market price previously acquired assets in a country whose currency has severely depreciated, most frequently due to prior inflationary excesses. But they cannot go on doing so indefinitely; and the experiences of recent years provides ample evidence that the market itself offers governments borrowing facilities which take account of the current value of gold and foreign exchange reserves which can be used as *de facto* or *de jure* collateral for such loans.

---

[8] C.f. particularly: the 'Documents relating to the European Monetary System' published in *European Economy*, No 12, July 1982.

4. External convertibility of the ECU

With regard to the convertibility of the ECU, the first thing to be stressed is that the 50 000 million ECUs held against gold and dollar deposits with the FECOM are as usable—and effectively used already—for settling deficits with countries outside the Community as dollars held directly in the United States.

Deficits with non-Community countries are indeed settled nearly exclusively in dollars, and entail a reduction *pari passu* of:

(i) the 20% of the dollar reserves held with the FECOM;

(ii) the 80% of the dollar reserves held outside the FECOM, principally on US commercial banks and in US Treasury notes.

From a strictly legal point of view, the external convertibility of these two types of reserves is therefore identical, and the pooling of reserves held with the FECOM does not entitle any country to draw on the reserves of another country. The dwindling international reserves of a country running persistent deficits will eventually force it into a devaluation of its currency, but this will not affect in any way the reserves of other participating countries.

This *automatic* convertibility does not apply to ECU holdings used to finance support operations for one or more currencies on the exchange market. Support operations of that nature have thus far been minimal, however (less than 1 500 million ECUs in April 1984). The global ceiling mechanism proposed earlier would prevent such operations proliferating to excess in the future, and continue to ensure that a reformed FECOM would retain the full capacity to honour the convertibility of its assets for the settlement of the same 20% of the foreseeable future external deficits of creditor countries, by drawing on no more than a very small fraction of its ample gold and dollar reserves.

The fact still remains, however, that the legal convertibility of ECUs into dollars would *not guarantee the stability* of the exchange rate at which that conversion will take place, no more than it would for the *national currency* of any individual participating country. But the likelihood of the dollar appreciating substantially from its current value against the ECU is certainly considerably less than that of a depreciation; and the strengthening of the EMS would open the way for greatly enhanced effectiveness of policies aimed at controlling those excessive (upwards or downwards) fluctuations in the dollar, which the Community considers to have an adverse impact; whatever else, it would also maintain an enhanced stability of their mutual exchange rates, which are of considerably more importance to them than the dollar rates.

5. Orientation of capital movements

One necessary prerequisite for maintaining the competitiveness of cross exchange-rates between Member States (see page 4) must be that any country—creditor or debtor—which considers a realignment of central rates to be preferable to the excessive growth of its claims or liabilities must be given the benefit of the doubt, particularly where persistant disequilibria in its current account can be attributed to significant *purchasing power differentials* between participating currencies, shown up in the painstaking—and admittedly only approximative—calculations made by economists.

Conversely, countries opposed to a currency realignment must also be awarded the benefit of the doubt whenever the strength or weakness of their currency on the exchange market cannot be blamed on such a disequilibrium, but is essentially due to movements of speculative capital. In that case, a search must be made for possible ways of avoiding pointless realignments which would be disequilibrating in the long- or even medium-run. And if that meant reverting to exchange controls—as foreseen in the Bretton Woods Agreement—then restrictions on the inflows of capital towards strong currencies would be an acceptable measure for such countries, reducing their fears of imported inflation and reinforcing the effectiveness of controls on capital outflows from deficit countries. Even preferable, of course, would be to institute market controls by way of improved coordination of interest rates and perhaps even an 'interest rate equalization tax' along the lines of that introduced in the United States in 1963, although this would clearly be difficult to implement and control.

This exploration of those possibilities should take into account the geographical constellation of disequilibrating capital movements, which today largely consist of massive shifts of capital between the United States and the rest of the world, [9] including Community countries. In this respect, it becomes particularly desirable that the Member States should coordinate their foreign exchange intervention policies and insist on closer negotiations with the US on matters of exchange rates, interest rates, etc.

Finally, the Community countries should also accept the principle that international credit facilities in general, and not just those provided by the FECOM, should not be used to finance the preservation of overvalued or undervalued exchange rates.

This principle should force:
* the deficit countries to consult their partners before they resort to international credit facilities, which means loans contracted on the market and from government authorities of foreign countries, just as much as those from the FECOM;
* the surplus countries to submit similarly to Community scrutiny the ways in which they propose to use those surpluses in the form of credits—and particularly by the building up of foreign exchange reserves by their central banks—to their partners within the Community, the United States and other countries. Has not the 'imported inflation' of which they justly complain too often been due to the excessive financing of countries other than those of the Community?

---

[9] Officially put at USD 41 000 million last year. The *Economic Outlook of the OECD* (July 1984, p. 61) predicts that they may reach USD 86 500 million this year rising to USD 105 000 million next year. More recent official US estimates would suggest that they may well exceed USD 100 000 million this year, to say nothing of the next.

6. Worldwide negotiations

All the issues developed in the foregoing pages—but particularly those dealing with exchange rates, interest rates and capital movements—are quite clearly issues of *world* concern, not peculiar to the Community alone. They are a matter for continuous negotiation—negotiations to which Jacques van Ypersele is by no means a stranger—with other countries including, first and foremost, the United States. The use of the dollar as a 'parallel world currency' signifies indeed that Community transactions, both on current and on capital account are *denominated and settled* in Community currencies or US dollars, but rarely in other foreign exchange. This enables the United States to run a colossal deficit on current account, financed by net inflows of capital. [10]

The cardinal sin to avoid would unquestionably be to delay the reforms of the EMS put forward by the authors of this book, and this preface, until such time as they can take account of an agreement reached with the US Administration; an eventuality which, unfortunately, seems to be still far too remote. To the contrary, in fact, the quickest way to reach such an agreement would be to push ahead with precisely those reforms. It is not enough to 'speak with one voice'. Indeed, is not one of the favourite slogans of all American negotiators and commentators that what they want to see is 'deeds, not words'!!

Worse still would be to allow the bolstering up of the ECU to be interpreted as an 'engine of war' against the dollar. The aim should not be to substitute the ECU for the dollar as a world reserve currency, but simply to offer a viable alternative to Eurodollars and other Eurocurrencies until such time as they can all give way to truly international monetary reserves deposited with the IMF, within the framework of a reformed world monetary system.

The United States must be shown that they have everything to gain by following the example of the EMS, and that the reinforcement of the EMS will enable the Community to cooperate more effectively with them in the search for a solution to commonly shared problems. The measures outlined above for restoring the stability of real exchange rates, bringing down interest rates, correcting budgetary deficits, etc., are unquestionably as much in the long-term interests of the United States as they are for the rest of the world. The short-run gains offered to the United States by excessively high interest rates and capital inflows financing its chronic and colossal budget deficits, combined with the insane and suicidal arms race under way on both sides of the Iron Curtain, do not add up to a lasting solution. Their continuation would be extremely costly to both the United States and the rest of the world.

---

[10] Failing more deep-rooted reform, could not a short-run solution be negotiated for appropriate compensatory capital exports by the United States in the spirit of the 'General Arrangements to Borrow' concluded in 1962 'to forestall or cope with an impairment of the international monetary system... in the new conditions of... greater freedom for short-term capital movements'?

7. Summary and conclusions

(*a*) It is high time that the Community States come to an agreement as to what they can do (1) in the long-term and (2) in the immediate future, to resolve the economic and monetary scandal which is the root cause of the '*infession*'—inflation followed by recession—which has held the world economy in its grip for more than a decade.

(*b*) The indispensable cooperation of the United States will remain unavailable as long as the Community countries fail to '*act* as one', rather than just '*speak* with a simple voice', and to prove to the United States that the reinforcement of the EMS is not 'an engine of war against the dollar', but is essentially designed to enhance the effectiveness of their own cooperation in working towards common goals.

(*c*) Pending a policy change on the part of the US Administration (as yet still too remote) the Community must do its utmost to create within Europe—and the rest of the world—an *oasis of stability* less at the mercy of the backwash effects of US policies and policy failures.

(*d*) Progress towards *Economic and Monetary Union* is vital in this respect and the real or imaginary sacrifices entailed for Member States by the necessary *mergers*—rather than *surrenders*—of national sovereignties (which have long been show rather than substance), are a far preferable alternative to the disasters entailed today by their lack of agreement on new Community policies and institutions.

(*e*) If the negotiations now in progress are to have any chance of success, then the legitimate fears of certain countries—and central banks in general—as to the inflationary dangers of ECU issues financing excessively lax policies of deficit countries and threatening the convertibility of the ECU, must be fully acknowledged and allayed.

The most appropriate measures in this respect are as much in the interests of deficit countries as they are in those of surplus countries. If their political leaders cannot impose those policies on their public opinion concerted—and, it is to be hoped, less substantial and less frequent—realignments of intra-Community central rates will at least enable them to fulfil the essential role of any foreign exchange system—i.e. the maintenance or speedy restoration of competitive real rates, in striking contrast, to the market fluctuations of a dollar which was vastly overvalued in the 1960s, undervalued in the 1970s, and once again overvalued today.

(*f*) The measures I have proposed constitute, I hope, a comprehensive package, the negotiation of which should be smoothed by numerous *quid pro quos* between the sacrifices called for and the benefits offered to the member countries.

But its success also calls for negotiators endowed with those rare qualities of vision, courage and tact amply demonstrated by Jacques van Ypersele de Strihou in the negotiation of the EMS.

Robert TRIFFIN
Louvain-la-Neuve

Contents

Introduction

The Heads of State or Government of the European Community countries decided to create a European Monetary System at the meeting of the *European Council* on 6 and 7 July 1978. Another session of the European Council, held in Brussels on 4 and 5 December 1978, defined the main principles of the EMS, which started operating on 13 March 1979. [1]

The EMS arose from *two complementary concerns.* First of all was the desire to establish—or rather to restore—some stability of exchange rates among European currencies, in a very unstable international environment, and thus to promote a continuing integration of Europe's national markets while improving the prospects of economic recovery. For, as we describe in Chapter I, the experience of flexible exchange rates—the 'floating' of the major currencies—has revealed that such stability was not a matter of course when the appropriate institutional framework and political will were missing.

But in addition the founders of the EMS intended that to this *external face* of monetary stability there should correspond an *internal face,* less visible though no less important.

Their objective was indeed that external stability be the result less of artificially imposed constraints than of a *convergence* of economic trends among member countries, in particular of prices and costs, as well as of a harmonization of their respective economic policies towards greater *internal* monetary stability.

The stabilization of exchange rates within the EMS, according to former Minister for Finance, Hans Matthöffer, in Germany, was not to be pursued for its own sake but would rather be 'the crystallization point of a community of stability'. [2] The desire to foster a convergence of the European economies toward greater internal monetary stability, especially by narrowing and lowering the range of inflation rates, was born of the bitter experience, undergone during the 1970s, of the detrimental results of inflation eventually on the rate of investment and thus of productivity, growth and employment.

This is the real meaning of the expression *zone of monetary stability in Europe* to which the closer monetary cooperation to be achieved by the EMS must lead, according

---

[1] See in Annex 2 the 'Founding acts' of the EMS, born of these two councils.
[2] Hans Matthöffer: 'Reden in der Feierstunde anläßlich des Wechsels in der Leitung der Deutschen Bundesbank, Frankfurt-am-Main, 20.12.1979', *Deutsche Bundesbank — Auszüge aus Presseartikeln*, No 2, 4.1.1980.

to the Bremen communiqué. It is in terms of this twofold objective that we must appraise the results of the EMS.

The creation of the EMS was not just the work of economic 'technicians' but also, to a great extent, *a political act*. It represented a new stage in the integration of economic policies and in the march toward European unity. In several countries the negotiations over the EMS gave rise to intense political debate.

The international political environment and Europe's potential role—and actual role—inspired the 1978 initiative by former President Giscard d'Estaing and former Chancellor Schmidt, and enabled them to overcome the reservations often expressed by 'technicians', especially within the Committee of the Governors of the Central Banks.

We will not analyse here the political debate which surrounded the creation of the EMS, nor the contingencies of both international and national politics which determined the time of its birth. The reader interested by this aspect could do no better, in our opinion, than turn to the excellent analysis by Peter Ludlow. [3]

Our first purpose is to outline the economic framework in which the creation of the EMS took place and to give the reasons for it (Chapter I). This initiative unfolded in a succession of efforts toward European monetary integration, the history of which is briefly told (Chapter II). Next we examine the EMS and describe the technical aspects of its mechanisms (Chapter III). We expand on this economic and technical framework with an analysis of the working of the EMS during its first five years, showing the strengths and weaknesses which practice has revealed (Chapter IV). Lastly, we give an account of some reforms and improvements that have been recently considered (Chapter V). At the conclusion of this survey the reader ought to have a better understanding of the role which the EMS can play in Europe's economic progress and of the manner in which it has until now fulfilled this task. We have no other ambition. [4]

---

[3] Peter Ludlow: *The Making of the European Monetary System*, Butterworth's European Studies, London, 1982.

[4] Along with the reading of the present book we recommend the excellent 'Documents relating to the European Monetary System', put together by the Commission of the European Communities and published in *European Economy*, No 12, July 1982.

Chapter I —
International motives
for the EEC initiative

The road to European monetary integration has been marked out by several previous efforts, but the setting up of the EMS to create a zone of monetary stability was an important step forward. It has contributed to the European Community's *internal development,* reflecting its ideals but also the conflicts over ends and means which have dogged its development. The next chapter briefly retells the history of the various attempts at European monetary integration, of which the EMS is the latest incarnation.

But the creation of the EMS—and to some extent of the monetary 'snake' which preceded it—also embodies a particular response to the problems posed by *changes in the international monetary system* and the world economy since the demise of the regime born in 1944 of the Bretton Woods agreement. For this demise, by opening the door to flexible exchange rates among major currencies, gave an empirical content to the prior academic debate over the merits of fixed versus flexible exchange rates in the adjustment process; new problems appeared, which were not foreseen or were deliberately minimized by the supporters of exchange rate flexibility, such as for instance the phenomenon which came to be known as 'overshooting' exchange rates. To these new challenges the EMS brings a certain type of response, and its creation thus finds its place within the general discussion over the respective merits of exchange rate fixity versus flexibility.

Finally, with the disappearance of the international monetary order which the Bretton Woods agreement had established for a quarter of a century, and with the aspiration for a new type of order, a new type of question has arisen. Should the reform of the international monetary system in order to create this new order be *world-wide,* or can it be achieved by way of *regional agreements* and by setting up zones of monetary stability? Thus the creation of the EMS also belongs to this other set of issues.

1. The debate over fixed or floating exchange rates [1]

(*a*) The return to a greater degree of exchange rate stability among European currencies came about largely as a result of a growing dissatisfaction with the operation of flexible exchange rates and with the great measure of instability it seemed to impart to foreign exchange markets. Such instability was felt to be harmful to investment and growth prospects in European economies and was perceived as a threat to European integration. The nature of this obstacle was described in the following terms by Alexandre Lamfalussy: 'no optimum allocation can take place unless market participants know with some degree of certainty the direction in which relative prices will move. But how could they have made any reasonable guesses about exchange rate movements with the kind of experience that we have had since 1973? The real cost of the present situation is, I fear, that decision-makers in the field of trade and investment have to concentrate an excessively large proportion of their energy on trying to guess exchange rate movements rather than on improving production processes, inventing new products and seeking out new markets'. [2]

But exchange rate flexibility is not necessarily by itself a cause of instability. Indeed, in some circumstances it seems to offer undeniable advantages over fixed exchange rates. To appreciate the reasons for the European initiative it is thus useful to recall the *main elements of the debate* over the degree of fixity or of flexibility which an international monetary system ought to have.

(*b*) When we study such a system, the first question that comes to mind concerns balance-of-payments disequilibria and what should be done in order to prevent them, or to correct them whenever they occur in the form of a surplus or a deficit. This is the problem technically known as the *adjustment process.*

In the Bretton Woods system, which well served the world economy for over 25 years, it was chiefly *internal measures,* of a monetary or budgetary nature, that were used to redress a temporary disequilibrium in a country's balance of payments. In case of a deficit, a more restrictive fiscal or monetary policy was prescribed. By reducing domestic demand, such a policy made more goods available for export while restraining imports, and the balance could thus be restored. The opposite policy of stimulating domestic demand was the way to deal with a surplus. Only in cases of fundamental and persisting disequilibrium could a country resort to an external solution and modify the official parity of its currency.

This system gave the world economy 25 years of relatively stable exchange rates and low inflation, setting the stage for an unprecedented growth of trade among nations. Its even-

---

[1] See J. van Ypersele: 'The European Monetary System: past experience and future prospects', in *The International Monetary System under Flexible Exchange Rates: Global, Regional and National,* edited by R. Cooper, P. Kenen, J. Braga de Macedo and J. van Ypersele, Ballinger Publishing Company, Cambridge, Massachusetts, 1982.

[2] A. Lamfalussy: 'A plea for an international commitment to exchange rate stability', Atlantic Institute for International Affairs, October 1981.

tual deterioration must be ascribed largely to the fact that the external adjustment process was not allowed to function properly. It operated with asymmetries which provoked excessive rigidity in exchange rates. Indeed, while countries (other than the United States) in a situation of fundamental deficit devalued their currencies in order to avoid further losses of reserves, countries in fundamental surplus refused to revalue theirs, in order to accumulate more reserves. As a result, the dollar became overvalued, causing a persistent deficit in the US balance of payments.

To be sure, the United States could have chosen to remedy this deficit by devaluing its own currency in relation to gold. But it was neither bound nor prompted to do so, given that the reserve currency status of the dollar permitted automatic financing of the US balance-of-payments deficit while satisfying the liquidity needs and the desire for reserve accumulation of the rest of the world. [3]

Whether the main responsibility for keeping an overvalued dollar must be imputed to the United States' desire to exploit to the full its advantageous reserve currency status, or to other countries' wish to accumulate dollar reserves by maintaining their balance of payments in fundamental surplus, the result was on both counts a world accumulation of dollar balances out of proportion with the other reserve asset, namely gold. This disproportion progressively undermined confidence in the dollar abroad and hastened its conversion into gold, leading to the setting up of a two-tier gold market in 1968 until the convertibility of the dollar had to be suspended in August 1971. [4]

From excessive rigidity in exchange rates one switched to the opposite extreme in 1973: an excess of flexibility following the generalized floating of the major currencies. This solution had long been in favour in academic circles, and its adoption in 1973 was hailed by many talented economists as a great step forward in international economic relations.

Since the arguments for flexible exchange rates still underlie most of the criticisms directed at exchange rate fixity in general and at the EMS in particular, they deserve careful consideration.

2. The theoretical advantages of flexible exchange rates

In a world like ours, made up of independent nations but interdependent national economies, exchange rate flexibility can in principle perform two vital functions: *adjustment* on the one hand and *insulation* on the other.

---

[3] See Anne O. Krueger: 'Current account targets and managed floating', in R.Z. Aliber, Ed., *The Political Economy of Monetary Reform*, 1978.

[4] This development, engraved in the logic of the Bretton Woods system, had been very correctly analysed and predicted by Robert Triffin as early as 1960 in his book *Gold and the Dollar Crisis*.

(*a*) In theory, the way flexible exchange rates allow adjustment to happen is as follows. For any balance-of-payments deficit, there must be, under any type of exchange rate regime, a corresponding demand for foreign exchange against national currency which exceeds the supply. If exchange rates are flexible—that is, if the central bank of the country in question does not intervene to satisfy at a fixed rate the excess demand for foreign exchange—the price of foreign exchange will go up as on any free market where the quantity demanded exceeds the quantity supplied. In other words, the exchange rate of the national currency will fall. This will result in a lowering of the prices of national products, expressed in foreign currency, in relation to foreign products. Exports will be stimulated and imports checked until equilibrium is restored. In the case of a balance-of-payments surplus, and thus of an excess supply of foreign exchange, the opposite movement will occur. The national currency will appreciate on the exchange market, which will reduce the competitiveness of national products against foreign goods.

To the first upholders of flexible exchange rates, this adjustment process through a variation of the exchange rate was to be swift and painless. [5] Internal measures of a monetary or fiscal nature would no longer be necessary for adjustment and could thus be guided only by domestic considerations of employment, growth and price stability.

Since, within a given country, the demand and supply of foreign exchange are much influenced by the country's macroeconomic policies in relation to other countries' policies, both through the effects of aggregate demand on imports and through the response of short-term capital flows to inter-country interest rate differentials, exchange rate flexibility would make compatible, to some extent, national economic policies that are normally pursued without much coordination.

By contrast, exchange rate fixity implies that some other adjustment mechanism—running down exchange reserves, deflating aggregate demand or controlling imports and capital outflows—must be brought into play whenever an excess demand for foreign exchange develops, thus obviously placing narrow constraints on the capacity of a country open to trade and capital movements to pursue domestic economic policy objectives.

(*b*) As to the *insulation* function performed by flexible exchange rates, it is obviously related to their capacity to restore equilibrium in the foreign exchange market. A country can afford to ignore external constraints and to pursue national economic objectives in a relatively autonomous manner precisely to the extent that the exchange rate mechanism takes care of external imbalances engendered by the pursuit of internal goals. Thus, for instance, a more expansionary policy than in one's trading partners must rapidly bring about growing trade deficits. Under a regime of fixed exchange rates, this might deplete the country's reserves, and possibly lead to the erection of protective barriers. Under flexible exchange rates, by contrast, the more rapid expansion can simply translate into a continuous depreciation of the country's currency *vis-à-vis* the currencies of countries where policy is less expansionary. By the same token, countries that are more attached to internal price stability can be insulated by an appreciating currency from the inflationary tendencies that might develop outside and would be likely to contaminate them under

---

[5] See for instance Milton Friedman, 'The case for flexible exchange rates', in *Essays in Positive Economics*, University of Chicago Press, Chicago, 1953.

exchange rate fixity. Thus, exchange rate flexibility was said to 'bottle up' inflation in the country where it arises. According to Milton Friedman's classic essay, flexible exchange rates 'are a means of permitting each country to seek monetary stability according to its own lights, without either imposing its mistakes on its neighbors or having their mistakes imposed on it'. [6]

In a world where rates of inflation have a tendency to diverge dramatically, as they did in the 1973 boom and subsequent episode of stagflation-recession, while balances of payments were sharply thrown into disequilibrium by the oil price increases, exchange rate flexibility played the role of a safety valve, failing which protectionist reactions would undoubtedly have been stronger.

More recently, prominent critics of the EMS and of the relative exchange rate fixity built into it have deplored the fact that countries with relatively stable prices, such as Germany, might be forced by EMS rules to accept a certain amount of imported inflation from their more inflationary partners in the EMS. Thus Dr Otmar Emminger, former president of the Deutsche Bundesbank, remarked that the experience of free floating, far from having an inflationary effect in Germany, shielded the country from imported inflation: 'Germany and Switzerland went over to floating in early 1973 not primarily with the aim of adjusting their payments balances but mainly in order to shield their monetary systems from destabilizing inflows of foreign exchange.' [7] This point will be developed further in Chapter III, section 6.

3. The drawbacks of flexible exchange rates in practice

It appears however that the practical experience of generalized floating among the major currencies was not very satisfactory and failed to establish once and for all the superiority of this system. Contrary to the expectations of its advocates, flexibility has been accompanied by much instability in exchange markets. Exchange rates have fluctuated much more widely than appeared to be warranted by underlying economic conditions and by inflation differentials. Furthermore balance-of-payments imbalances, far from being swiftly eliminated, have remained on the average very large since 1973. How is it possible to reconcile this disappointing practice with the hopes that theoretical speculation on the virtues of flexible exchange rates had raised?

(a) First of all it appears that the *adjustments did not take place in the manner predicted* by simple theoretical models focused on the trade balance. Flows of international trade appear to be influenced only slowly by exchange rate variations, but react rapidly to variations in aggregate demand. This is borne out by a number of empirical studies. [8] Moreover, in recent circumstances where trade deficits were mostly due to oil-price

---

[6] Friedman, op. cit.
[7] Otmar, Emminger: 'Remarks at a conference of the American Enterprise Institute in Washington on 28.2.1980', *Deutsche Bundesbank — Auszüge aus Presseartikeln*, No 28, 27.3.1980.
[8] See Marc A. Miles: 'The Effects of Devaluation on the Trade Balance and the Balance of Payments', *Journal of Political Economy*, Vol. 87, No 3, June 1979.

increases, exchange rate variations are an even less effective means of adjustment, given the low price-elasticity of the demand for crude oil in the short run. It can be argued that more emphasis should be laid on adjustment by means of internal economic measures.

Of course, such evidence is not enough to invalidate the case for flexible exchange rates. One can still claim that exchange rate variations will be effective for adjustment if they are accompanied by the right supporting measures bearing on aggregate demand. In countries with a chronic external deficit and a high rate of inflation, currency depreciation can presumably produce the desired results if it is accompanied by measures to restrain aggregate demand and control the money supply. Conversely, an appreciation of the currency can eliminate a balance-of-payments surplus if it goes hand in hand with expansionary measures at home.

The question then becomes whether such accompanying measures, which are necessary for adjustment in any case, are likely to be taken in case of a spontaneous variation of the exchange rate in a regime of flexibility. The record of the recent experience leaves one sceptical on that score. As Henry Wallich put it concisely: 'The promise of speedy adjustment of payment imbalances through exchange rate movements has remained unfulfilled, perhaps because the very ease with which exchange rates could move has diminished political pressure to adopt appropriate fiscal and monetary policies'.[9] By contrast, when exchange rates are stable but adjustable, their variation, though more difficult to achieve because it requires a conscious decision by the political power, possibly to be taken in concert with the governments of the partner countries as in the EMS, is thereby more likely to be accompanied by the fiscal and monetary measures as well as the incomes policies which will guarantee its effectiveness. Such a system would therefore allow one, better than flexible exchange rates do, to use a variation of the exchange rate as an economic policy instrument.[10] As we shall see in Chapter IV, the experience of the latest monetary realignments within the EMS has brought encouragement on this score.

Along the same lines, it has been argued that a change in the exchange rate will be effective for adjustment provided it leads to a real (as opposed to nominal) change in the value of the exchange rate and thus is not offset by an increase of the inflation differential between the country and the rest of the world. (It is obvious that if, following a 10% nominal depreciation of a currency relative to another, prices in the first country increase on the average by 10% relative to prices in the second country, the real exchange rate between the two currencies will be back to the level it had before the depreciation occurred.) But, as we shall see, such offsetting movements in the form of 'vicious' or 'virtuous' circles have shown a tendency to appear under exchange rate flexibility, especially in small open economies.

(b) A crucial factor in altering the role of exchange rate changes in balance-of-payments adjustment has been the *growing importance of short-term capital movements.* Few economists imagined 20 years ago that such movements would come to dominate the

---

[9] Henry C. Wallich: 'Exchange Rates, Inflation and the Dollar', *Impact*, No 30, 1980/2.
[10] See on this point the comments made by C. W. McMahon in *US-European Monetary Relations*, edited by Samuel I. Katz, AEI Institute, Washington DC, 1977.

foreign exchange market to such an extent that eventually they would almost completely eclipse trade transactions. This phenomenon kept pace with the growing internationalization of economic relations during the 1960s. It gathered momentum in the 1970s, for the accidents of geology and of political geography have placed a great many oil-fields in countries with a low population density, so that those countries controlled financial assets which sometimes much exceeded their developmental needs. The bulk of this capital is in search of short-term investments, and its holders are more and more anxious to diversify their portfolio of liquid assets, especially in terms of the currencies in which these assets are denominated.

Furthermore, for several years after the first oil shock, the United States increased rather than diminished its dependence on imported petroleum. This helped maintain the rapid accumulation of dollar balances in the world while contributing to the important depreciation of the dollar which took place between 1974 and 1980. These phenomena have naturally intensified the desire to diversify currency reserves, both public and private.

The fact that asset markets react much more rapidly than the flows of trade, so that exchange rate variations are more and more often determined by portfolio adjustments, is undoubtedly behind the prevalence of the phenomenon of 'overshooting', which can occur in the following way. Under flexible exchange rates, a country whose currency appreciates because of, for instance, a favorable current account balance, will not necessarily see its trade surplus being corrected very fast by the exchange rate appreciation. (On the contrary, it is quite possible in a first stage that the trade surplus of a country whose currency appreciates increases further: this is known as a J-curve effect.) But this country is likely to attract in the meantime short-term foreign capital which speculates on the chances of a further appreciation. The surplus which subsequently appears in the balance of capital flows will in effect cause a new appreciation, thus confirming *ex post* the speculators' expectations. The reverse phenomenon can of course occur in a country whose currency initially depreciates because of a deficit on current account.

(*c*) Such *capital mobility,* coupled with the tendency of asset markets to adjust more rapidly than goods markets, is thus what explains the phenomenon of 'overshooting' exchange rates but in addition *reduces the degree of the insulation* which exchange rate flexibility was supposed to provide.

Indeed, let us imagine a country that takes advantage of the 'licence to inflate', or to reflate, its economy which exchange rate flexibility supposedly gives. Let us suppose that, as a result, this country sees its inflation rate rise above its partners' and lets its currency depreciate on the exchange market accordingly.

Phenomena of destabilizing speculation and of overadjustment will then provoke a currency depreciation which exceeds the initial increase of the country's rate of inflation over its partners'. But the rising prices of imported goods will feed the inflationary process, and a vicious spiral of depreciation-inflation will begin. Thus, excessive variations of the exchange rate—in excess, that is, of the inflation differential—will tend to be accommodated *ex post* by a supplementary increase in the level of internal prices. [11]

---

[11] In *Gold and the Dollar Crisis*, op cit. pp. 82-83, R. Triffin already analysed the likelihood of such phenomena and the limits they set to the efficiency of an exchange rate variation for adjustment.

Small, open economies will in general be more sensitive to such contagion, essentially for the following reasons. First of all they are, more than larger countries, likely to face both a supply of imported goods which is very elastic at the world price, given their small share in the total consumption of these goods, and a domestic demand for the same goods which is rather inelastic, in view of their weaker capacity to substitute national products for these goods. Thus a change in the exchange rate will in small countries translate into a change in import prices, expressed in national currency, which on the average is greater than in larger countries. [12] In addition, a change in import prices will affect internal price formation more in small open economies than in large countries, to the extent that in such economies imports of final goods represent a greater share of domestic consumption and of input use in domestic production. In the European Community, the degree of openness of the economies, expressed by the value of imports of goods and services as a share of the total of final expenditures, was in 1982 41% for Belgium, 37% for Ireland, 35% for the Netherlands, 26% for Denmark, between 25 and 20% for the Federal Republic of Germany, Greece, Italy, France and the United Kingdom. In the United States and in Japan, the figures are 10% and 14% respectively.

In conclusion it can be said that, under flexible exchange rates, short-term capital movements make it difficult for a country to keep under control an inflationary process which, under fixed exchange rates, would at least be disciplined by the external constraint. Thus the freedom to pursue a more expansionary policy than one's partners under the false protection of a flexible exchange rate may rapidly turn into an uncontrollable addiction! [13] The fear of being thrown into such vicious circles, coupled with a growing recognition of the ineffectiveness of exchange rate variations, when unaided, in correcting fundamental disequilibria, helps explain the member countries' attachment to the EMS as a system of stable but adjustable parities as well as the fact that, increasingly, concerted parity readjustments in the EMS are accompanied by the internal measures aimed at making them effective.

4. The debate on reforming the international monetary system and the question of regional agreements

The problem of reforming the international monetary system had already arisen under the fixed exchange rate regime of the Bretton Woods agreement, as the disadvantages of too much rigidity appeared with increasing clarity. The move to the other extreme—that is, of too much flexibility in exchange relationships—did not erase the problem, even if it had the effect of making previous reform proposals redundant.

---

[12] See Peter B. Kenen and Clare Pack: 'Exchange rates, Domestic Prices and the Adjustment process', *Group of Thirty*, Occasional Paper, No 1, 1980.

[13] Over this problem and its manifestation in European countries during the 1970s, the reader can profitably turn to the developments contained in the 'Documents relating to the EMS', op. cit. pp. 21-22. See also the more theoretical analysis by Pentti Kouri in 'Macroeconomics of stagflation under flexible exchange rates', *The American Economic Review*, Vol. 72, No 2, May 1982.

The current search for a third solution, halfway between too much rigidity and too much flexibility, begins from the following conclusions.

On the one hand, exaggerated fluctuations in exchange rates may increase the mood of uncertainty in business circles and upset the development of foreign trade. In addition, as we have seen, they may complicate the task of economic policy-makers through the interference of potentially destabilizing factors, particularly in small countries with open economies.

On the other hand, going back to a universal system of fixed parities in the foreseeable future would be practically impossible, given the importance, since the Bretton Woods era, of international capital movements.

One is thus led to the conclusion that a gradual return to greater international monetary stability should comprise two elements:
(i) First, the creation throughout the world of a few large zones of monetary stability inside which the harmonization of economic policies would promote more stable exchange rates;
(ii) Secondly, an attempt to reduce the frequency and the amplitude of exchange rate fluctuations between these large zones, while securing a high level of economic activity through a better coordination of demand management policies, especially on the monetary and the fiscal plane.

In the present state, the construction of this new world monetary order could encompass three zones: a European zone, a yen zone and a dollar zone. The necessity to achieve a better coordination of economic policies among these three zones and to strive together for a better control of exchange rate fluctuations among their currencies compels growing recognition. The Versailles Summit of the great industrial countries and of the European Community in June 1982 revealed a greater awareness of this need.

The seven Heads of State or Government, as well as the representatives of the European Community who gathered in Versailles, have in particular made clear their intention to 'work towards a constructive and orderly evolution of the international monetary system by a closer cooperation among the authorities representing the currencies of North America, of Japan and of the European Community in pursuing medium-term economic and monetary objectives'. They have subscribed to a 'statement of international monetary undertakings' (the text of which appears in Annex 3) in which they 'accept a joint responsibility to work for greater stability of the world monetary system'. This is to be achieved, in particular, by further harmonizing economic policies, strengthening cooperation with the IMF in its surveillance, and intervening in exchange markets to counter disorderly conditions. This international commitment was renewed at the Summits which came after Versailles but has not so far, it appears, produced any concrete results nor led to any significant dampening of the fluctuations among major currencies.

5. The motives behind the European initiative [14]

A basic economic motive behind the creation of the EMS was, as we have seen, the dissatisfaction with the experience of floating exchange rates and the conviction that this monetary situation was harmful to European integration and detrimental to employment and growth in Europe.

The recent 'Documents relating to the European Monetary System', published by the European Commission, emphasizes this point: 'The development of international trade, and in particular of intra-Community trade, has been based to a large extent on exchange rate stability. It is difficult to imagine how frontiers could have been opened up and common policies established at European level if there had not been a substantial degree of certainty about economic variables as important as the relative prices of currencies. This achievement must be safeguarded and reinforced. The adoption of protectionist policies and the fragmentation of capital markets would turn the present stagnation into a deep depression aggravated by an international financial crisis. Growing commercial and financial interdependence is an enormous asset, but it implies responsibilities, which are themselves growing, towards other countries especially in the area of exchange rates.' [15]

Expressed more positively, the primary objective of the EMS is thus to promote European economic integration and to improve lastingly the growth performance and the employment prospects of the Community, by way of the greater exchange rate stability and the convergence toward internal stability this implies. This objective will be met only if the system is sufficiently robust and credible, and also if it is biased toward neither inflation nor deflation.

(a) The EMS can promote a *greater stability in exchange rates* at two levels:
(i) in the short term, by ironing out excessive fluctuations;
(ii) in the long term, by encouraging a better convergence of Member States' economies.

1. Short-term stability

Through its rules for intervention and its credit mechanism, which will be described later on, the EMS should effectively counter 'overshooting', that is changes in exchange rates in excess of what inflation differentials would suggest. Such phenomena have often occurred in the past. They can originate inside the economic and monetary region which they affect. They can also be initiated by movements of third currencies, particularly the dollar.

---

[14] See J. van Ypersele: 'Prospects for European Monetary Integration', in *Europe and the Dollar in the World-Wide Disequilibrium*, edited by J.R. Sargent, 1981.
[15] Op. cit.

At times where a lack of confidence drives dollar holders to move 'out of' the dollar and 'into' other currencies, this asset diversification does not benefit all European currencies uniformly. Often it singles out one particular currency, which is the German mark. This results in pushing up the German mark, in raising its tension with other European currencies, and possibly worsening the competitive position of German products in foreign markets. The support given by Chancellor Schmidt to the EMS creation derived partially from his desire to mitigate these inconveniencies by spreading out over a larger zone the impact of a weak dollar, in an era (1977-78) when the Germans found this weakness particularly preoccupying. [16]

To express the same idea in the economists' jargon, one can say that exchange rates between great currencies have often been determined by 'portfolio adjustments'. The resulting exchange rate variations have often overshot the purchasing-power parity level between these large currencies themselves, as well as between these currencies and other currencies which are less extensively used as instruments for reserve or for financial investment. Such excessive movements in the exchange rate can be accommodated *ex post* by variations in internal prices—the more so the more open the economies are—and thus tend to exacerbate inflation differentials.

The EMS exchange mechanism, with its obligation to intervene when certain margins are reached, and with the resources it makes available to finance such intervention, should help prevent these 'overshooting' movements.

2. Longer-term stability

There is of course a more fundamental way for the system to contribute to greater exchange rate stability. Participation in the EMS supposes that, in the adjustment process, member countries will give preference to internal policy measures over exchange rate variations. Should this not be the case, the system would rapidly cease to operate effectively. Participating countries therefore must understand and admit that, by adhering to this system, they accept the obligation to strive for a greater convergence of their basic stances of internal economic policy.

This is sometimes called the disciplining element of the system, but such terminology is misleading insofar as it can give the impression that the obligation to adjust necessarily implies restrictive measures that would only apply to deficit countries. On the contrary, adjustments should take place with a certain amount of symmetry, with surplus countries contributing by expansionary measures to the achievement of general convergence. This ideal of symmetry is embodied in some of the EMS mechanisms, as we shall see later.

(b) A greater stability of exchange relationships should *improve growth and employment prospects* in several ways.

1. Firstly, it should allow a *more sustained expansion of demand, both foreign and domestic,* to take place. For monetary instability in Europe is felt to have had a defla-

---

[16] Peter Ludlow, *The Making of the European Monetary System,* op. cit. pp. 71-73.

tionary impact at certain times. In some countries, an excessive appreciation of the currency gave rise to deflationary pressures by checking sales and reducing profits in export industries. This was one of the causes of the slowing down of economic growth in the Federal Republic of Germany in 1977 and 1978.

On the other hand, in countries where the currency depreciated too much *vis-à-vis* the strong currencies, the downward overshooting intensified the inflationary pressures through increased import prices and wage indexation mechanisms. These inflationary consequences of depreciation can check the economic recovery: the countries so affected prevent their economies from growing too fast out of fear of the pressures this might produce on their balances of payments and of the renewed risk of further depreciation and inflation.

Greater monetary stability should have a positive influence on economic recovery by allowing demand to expand at a faster rate. This would produce important multiplier effects in view of the degree of openness of European economies and of the importance of intra-EEC trade in the total: trade with the European partners thus approximately represents 70% of Belgium's foreign trade, 50% for France and Germany, and 40% for the United Kingdom and Italy.

2. Greater monetary stability would also strengthen business confidence and reactivate investment. European business executives have often complained how difficult it is to give their enterprises a fully European dimension in view of the exchange risks and of the uncertainty about inflation rates. These twin phenomena do not make for easy forecasting of the cost in national currency of imported inputs, or of the revenue in national currency from foreign sales. Undoubtedly this uncertainty contributes to the fact that firms do not reap all the potential benefits which a market the size of Europe offers. It also has a paralysing effect on investment and reinforces protectionist pressures.

The advocates of flexible exchange rates like to point out, in opposition to our case, that surveys of opinions of firms engaged in international operations do not reveal that they feel handicapped by exchange rate flexibility. [17] In addition, most econometric studies done so far do not indicate that the level of foreign trade was significantly affected by exchange rate instability.

One has to reply, though, that those opinion surveys over-represent multinational corporations, and that the size of such firms allows them to reduce their exchange risk exposure and even in some cases, as a by-product of their principal activity, to speculate profitably on the foreign exchange market. [18] Moreover, these surveys show that if business firms do not object to flexibility *per se*, they heartily dislike the volatility which is so often associated with it. Lastly, as it was pointed out in a study by the IMF, neither opinion surveys nor econometric studies answer the question whether exchange rate instability does or does not lead to poor resource allocation. Indeed, 'Exchange rate instability might lead some firms to seek a reduction of their exchange rate exposure by (i) setting up separate production units in each of their major national markets so as to

---

[17] See *Group of Thirty:* 'Foreign exchange markets under floating rates', 1980.
[18] See the article by David Marsh: 'Sheikhs of the currency markets', *Financial Times*, 24.5.1982.

minimize the risk of sudden movements in the ratio of costs to product prices; and by (ii) importing more from countries to which they are exporting, or by exporting more to the countries from which they are importing. In all these cases, it is clear that the decrease in the volume of international trade could be small, but that the move away from a full exploitation of the comparative advantages of the various countries could be quite significant.' [19]

Let us point out that, contrary to previous econometric investigations, a recent study of US-German trade between 1977 and 1981 came to the conclusion that 'exchange rate variability reduces the volume of international trade in manufactured goods.' [20]

In conclusion, it can be presumed that exchange rate instability has managed to replace, at least partially, ancient customs barriers and to exert the same detrimental influence on the growth and development of an extensive European market. The dismantling of customs barriers was one of the factors behind accelerating European growth during the 1960s. The story of the attempts at monetary integration in Europe, which are the subject of the next chapter, clearly shows the need for, but also the difficulty of, accomplishing economic integration, which otherwise will constantly be threatened by the subtle form of impediment to trade that exchange rate instability entails.

---

[19] IMF: *International aspects of policies of monetary restraint*, 2.11.1981, p. 31.
[20] See 'Effects of exchange rate uncertainty on German and US trade', M.A. Akhtar and R. Spence Hilton, *Federal Reserve Bank of New York Quarterly Review*, Spring 1984.

Chapter II — The ebb and flow of European monetary integration

To understand the mechanisms of the EMS (Chapter III) and its operation until now (Chapter IV), some history is useful. The EMS was, after all, preceded by other attempts at monetary integration—or in any case monetary coordination—in the European Economic Community. Some of those attempts did not go beyond ideas, others took shape in the 'monetary snake', still others had some of their elements incorporated in the EMS. Moreover, the difficulties which those first attempts addressed and the new obstacles they occasionally encountered, often anticipated the current problems of the EMS. For these reasons, it is appropriate to retrace briefly their history. (Annex I contains, in addition, the *timetable* of events which had important monetary implications for the EEC.)

1. The main factors in the story

The story of the attempts which culminated in the EMS is not one of smooth progress. Times which were rich in achievements, or at least in ambitious proposals, have been followed by slack periods during which the goal of monetary integration appeared to be dormant. This somewhat chaotic evolution can be explained by factors that are both internal and external to the European Community. They can be summarized as follows.

Internally, there seems to be a kind of *cumulative logic of integration* [1] by virtue of which market integration—the creation of a real common market—eventually calls for monetary integration as its natural extension. This is because the integration of markets makes economies more and more interdependent. Thus, for the six original EEC partners, the share of intra-EEC trade in total foreign trade went up from 30% in 1958 to 50% in 1972. In addition, a growing freedom of capital movements in the integrated area almost necessarily goes hand in hand with a broadening of national firms' operations to the scale of the common market.

This growing interdependence of the economies increases both the risks and the size of balance-of-payments disequilibria. It is likely, moreover, to reduce the efficiency of national economic policies in the pursuit of domestic goals. A consequence of the great

---

[1] This expression is borrowed from Loukas Tsoukalis: *The Politics and Economics of European Monetary Integration*, London 1977. Much inspiration for the following paragraphs was derived from this book.

openness of the economies will be to dissipate externally—and to transfer onto the balance of payments—a good part of the effect of expanding or contracting domestic demand that an autonomous fiscal policy might seek. Capital mobility makes monetary policy less and less effective, since it will have the effect of offsetting by inflows or outflows of capital each autonomous attempt to contract or expand the monetary stock in a single country.

Let us note in passing that the signatories of the Treaty of Rome had subscribed to the principle of freedom for capital movements (Article 3) and had agreed that restrictions to such movements would gradually be removed to the extent that was needed for the proper functioning of the common market. Until now the attainment of this objective has been far from complete. Some Member States have, for all practical purposes, freed their national capital markets. But others have adopted new controls or restored old controls they had lifted in the early 1960s. Moreover, the development of Eurocurrency transactions, falling outside the national authorities' purview, was a powerful factor in liberating capital movements in the Community. The expansion of Euromarkets may or may not have rendered obsolete the goal of integrating national financial markets as it was defined in the Treaty of Rome,[2] but their existence certainly puts obvious constraints on the capacity of national monetary authorities to pursue independent policies.

Thus the cumulative logic of integration seems to force national economies into one of the following options:

(i) either to reduce their interdependence via protectionist measures;

(ii) or to reconcile national independence with economic interdependence by adopting flexible exchange rates. This was the solution that increasingly prevailed among great currencies during the 1970s, though we saw in the previous chapter that there are limits to the autonomy which this 'insulation' can provide, particularly for small countries;

(iii) or, lastly, to step forward on the road of integration and to restore the effectiveness of fiscal and monetary policies over the integrated space by coordinating them more fully or even by entrusting a supranational authority with their charge. This last solution appears to be the logical final outcome of the integration process of European economies which began 25 years ago.

Evidently this cumulative logic, which the pressure of economic events can sometimes make compelling, will at other times run into a strong reluctance to accept its political and institutional implications by deepening the integration. Two lines of argument collide in this respect, and continue to collide in current debates on the necessary convergence within the EMS (see Chapters IV and V). Some will insist upon a harmonization of national economic policies as a precondition for any institutional form of monetary integration, failing which, they claim, Member States that usually have a balance-of-payments surplus could very well be forced into granting automatic financing to Member States that are chronically in deficit, without being able to exert a disciplining influence upon them. Others think instead that an institutionalized system of monetary integration can put sufficient pressure on countries in deficit, and that the progress of monetary

---

[2] This question is discussed in Chapter 8 of the 'Annual Economic Review 1982-83' of the Commission of the European Communities, published in *European Economy*, No 14, November 1982.

integration will by itself foster a deeper coordination and harmonization of national policies.

The *external influences* behind the proposals for European monetary integration have undoubtedly been the development of the international monetary system and the opinions formed on this subject. So long as the Bretton Woods regime, based upon fixed parities, seemingly performed well and was accompanied by a gradual liberalization of capital movements, the specific need for deeper forms of monetary integration in a European framework did not arise, the more so because such a framework would not have included the system's two great reserve currencies, namely sterling and the dollar.

But as soon as questions arose about the system's viability, and signs of destabilization began to appear (e.g. in the sterling crisis of 1967), the idea of establishing in Europe a zone of monetary stability, and of thus protecting European economies from the turbulence which the demise of the Bretton Woods system could not fail to provoke, could acquire greater appeal. More recently, in an international environment that repeatedly signalled its instability and its fragility, the notion that European Community countries could collectively reduce their vulnerability and sensitivity to outside influences by means of monetary integration seems to have motivated the proponents of the EMS. [3]

Lastly, ever since the reform of the international monetary system has been on the agenda, initiatives of monetary integration in Europe can also be viewed as a stage in a possible strategy of reform which would rest upon promoting regional agreements (see Chapter I, section 4). The nature of opinion towards this strategy inevitably influences how such efforts are perceived.

2. A résumé of European monetary integration from the Treaty of Rome to the European Summit of the Hague in 1969

(*a*) Economic integration can be pursued negatively, by the elimination of impediments to trade. It can also be pursued in a more positive fashion by developing common intervention and policies. While the stipulations of the Rome Treaty are rather precise and compelling with regard to the first type of integration, they are much less so on the subject of common policies, expressing little more than a fairly vague agreement on general objectives, which are spelled out in Articles 103 to 108 of the Treaty of Rome.

(i)   Article 103 states that short-term economic policy should be considered a matter of common interest and form the subject of mutual consultations.

(ii) Article 104 prescribes that each Member State should follow policies that will ensure the equilibrium of its balance of payments, maintain confidence in the value of its currency, and foster a high degree of employment and of price stability.

(iii) Article 105 lays down the principle of a coordination of economic policies in order to

---

[3] See Peter Ludlow: *The making of the European Monetary System*, op. cit. p. 91.

attain the objectives set forth in the preceding article. A Monetary Committee with consultative status is created in order to promote the coordination of monetary policies.

(iv) Article 106 stipulates that exchange controls should be lifted along with the growing liberalization in the movements of goods, persons and capital that will follow from the application of the Treaty.

(v) Article 107 prescribes that the rate of exchange of each currency shall be considered a matter of common interest.

(vi) Article 108 introduces the possibility of mutual assistance in case of serious balance-of-payments difficulties.

While the principles thus stated can accommodate very deep forms of positive integration, they do not provide for any concrete steps leading there. This caution on the part of the Treaty of Rome's authors probably was, to a large extent, an expression of political realism. The agreement on forming a customs union among the Six had been laboriously obtained, against the preference expressed by some for the formula of a 'free-trade area', which the United Kingdom had proposed and which represented a form of looser integration but aimed at a broader area. If the supporters of tighter integration had tried to go beyond what had been obtained, by demanding more specific commitments on positive integration and economic policy coordination, they would have run the risk of destroying even the consensus that was attained.

Moreover it was well known that the ideas over what economic policy ought to be, and more particularly over the optimal degree of State intervention in the economy, greatly differed among Member States, making any attempt to define a common policy unworkable. Thus it was more realistic and feasible to focus the precise commitments on the process of negative integration, and to restrict positive integration to the affirmation of general principles.

Lastly, it should be borne in mind that the creation of the European Economic Community took place in a context of international monetary stability. The Bretton Woods system, based on fixed parities and on the gold-exchange standard, was at the time not in dispute. Therefore it was nearly unthinkable to set up in the EEC an independent monetary system that would have left out the dollar and sterling. If the need for monetary cooperation arose, the type of cooperation one naturally thought of was 'Atlantic'—thus including the United States and the United Kingdom—rather than European.

(b) Nevertheless, the first attempts to transcend the somewhat vague stipulations of the Rome Treaty on European monetary cooperation were inspired more by external considerations—the development of the international monetary system—than by the Community's internal development. In his book *Gold and the Dollar Crisis*, published in 1960, Professor *Robert Triffin* clearly described the defects of the Bretton Woods system and correctly predicted the manner of its demise. He also proposed a plan leading by stages to the creation of a European monetary union and of a common currency. Less ambitious, though proceeding from a kindred inspiration, was a proposal, made in 1959 by the Belgian Minister for Foreign Affairs, *Pierre Wigny,* to adopt a European unit of account which would be the first sign of the financial role that the Community intended to play on the international monetary scene.

But, internally, monetary cooperation did not appear as an urgent problem, particularly since every one of the six Community countries had a balance-of-payments surplus between 1958 and 1961 (with the exception of France in 1958). There did not seem to be any payments disequilibrium within the Community.

Attitudes changed, however, in the wake of the 5% revaluations of the mark and of the guilder on 6 and 7 March 1961. These readjustments, motivated by the important payments surpluses of Germany and the Netherlands with countries outside the European Community, were decided without any European consultation. They thus raised the double problem, still with us, of the sensibility of intra-EEC exchange relationships to external pressures and of the absence of a common European policy to deal with them.

Following these events, the Monetary Committee issued a report calling for a greater stability of exchange rates within the Community and for a closer coordination of economic and monetary policies. The Commission drew inspiration from these injunctions with its 'Community's action programme during the second stage of the common market', which came out at the end of 1962. In the monetary domain, the Commission attempted to fill the gaps in the Rome Treaty by proposing concrete stages that would lead to the establishment of a monetary union. For the second stage of the transitional period (due to end in 1970) the Commission proposed the setting up of a Committee of the Governors of the Central Banks, a Committee for Budgetary Policy and a Committee for Medium-term Economic Policy, as well as the adoption of a system of preliminary consultations for all important monetary policy decisions, the creation of a system of mutual assistance and the further liberalization of capital movements.

Some of these recommendations, and more particularly those aiming at the creation of three committees in order to institutionalize concerted action, were adopted by the EEC Council of Ministers in 1964. Member States pledged in addition not to modify henceforth the parity of their currency without a preliminary consultation of their partners, thus applying the principle of Article 107 of the Rome Treaty. The adoption of these reforms in 1964 was probably accelerated by the balance-of-payments crisis which Italy suffered in 1964, accompanied by a large inflow of speculative capital into the FR of Germany. This crisis was the first manifestation of a serious disequilibrium existing within the Community and of the Community's incapacity to deal with it. To finance her external deficit, Italy turned for help to the United States and the IMF rather than to her European partners.

In its 'action programme' the Commission also put forward proposals for a third stage on the road to monetary union, during which exchange rates among European currencies would become irrevocably fixed and a European reserve currency would be created. These latter proposals, inasmuch as they engaged the Community's future in a very precise direction, were coolly received, especially in Germany. German leaders feared lest the creation of a European monetary block should be detrimental to the Atlantic monetary cooperation they continued to favour. They also feared that this might unduly provoke an increase of international monetary liquidity and a relaxation of the discipline which the balance-of-payments constraint imposed on national governments.

(c) In the history of European monetary integration, the years from 1964 to 1968 may appear as a slack period. There are several reasons for this absence of progress. Paradoxically, one of the reasons was further integration in other areas, since the birth of the common agricultural policy (CAP), by making parity changes much more difficult, entailed for a time the illusion that the European monetary union existed *de facto*.

Indeed, one of the rules of the common agricultural policy is the unity of agricultural prices in the EEC, achieved by fixing prices each year in European units of account (defined in relation to gold and created in 1962) for all the agricultural products subject to the intervention regime.

The agreement on fixing common prices for cereals in units of account dates from December 1964. It normally implied that henceforth prices of cereals, once expressed in national currency, were to increase by the percentage of devaluation in the country which devalued its currency, or decrease by the percentage of revaluation in the country which revalued its currency. This would have produced serious disadvantages. In the country which devalued its currency farmers would be unilaterally favoured, overproduction encouraged and inflationary tensions rekindled. In the country which revalued its currency, farmers would be penalized. Thus the common agricultural policy became a serious obstacle to parity changes, since any change of parity might well have jeopardized the principles on which the CAP was built.

In this particular episode of the 'cumulative logic of integration', the reticence formerly expressed by Germany and the Netherlands about a definitive fixing of parities continued but weakened somewhat. On the other hand, countries like France, which profited from the common agricultural policy most, came naturally to support the Commission's proposal to fix exchange rates and create a European currency. Thus monetary union appeared once again to be the logical extension of the integration process.

Furthermore, monetary union seemed to many to be achieved *de facto*, with exchange rates inside the Community permanently stabilized. Supplementary institutional initiatives thus seemed superfluous.

The other major reason for the lack of institutional progress in monetary integration during that period was the dominant problem of reforming the international monetary system, which monopolized the Monetary Committee's attention for most of the time.

This is not the place to recall the vicissitudes which surrounded those discussions. One should remember however, that the six European partners failed to adopt a common attitude on the reform of the international monetary system, General de Gaulle's government in France having unambiguously expressed its preference for a return to the gold standard, while the other five members of the European Community sought to improve the existing system of the gold-exchange standard rather than to replace it.

Politics evidently carried a great weight in a debate which was not simply a technicians' concern. The French preference probably reflected a strategy of independence, pursued on several fronts, from what was perceived as the hegemony of the United States, especially in the monetary field.

36

The debate on the monetary questions also became politicized as a result of the British request to enter the EEC, opposed by France in part on the grounds of weakness of the pound sterling (which devalued by 14.3% on 18 November 1967). A strengthening of monetary integration among the six European partners could thus be pursued, either as an additional barrier to the United Kingdom's entry, or instead as a framework in which a future integration of the British currency could more easily take place.

(d) At the beginning of 1968, the Prime Minister of Luxembourg *Pierre Werner* issued a *plan for action* which contained, among other proposals, the irrevocable fixing of exchange rates between Community currencies, the European unit of account and the European Monetary Fund. This plan was followed with a memorandum by the Commission—the first *'Barre plan'* (Mr Raymond Barre being at the time the Commission's Vice-President) which on some points retreated from Mr Werner's ideas. It nevertheless proposed, in addition to extending the procedures for preliminary consultation and to strengthening the convergence of the economies:

(i)   to set up a Community system of short-term monetary support and of medium-term financial assistance;

(ii) to subject decisions on parity changes to the preliminary agreement (and no longer simply the preliminary consultation) of other Member countries;

(iii) to examine the possibility of a complete suppression of fluctuation margins between European currencies.

Other events conspired at that time to reawaken interest in European monetary integration, mostly by revealing how wanting it was. We have already mentioned the United Kingdom's request to adhere to the Treaty of Rome. The political turmoil that the May 1968 events provoked in France was also followed by a monetary crisis, and by pressures for revaluing the mark and for devaluing the French franc (which the German and French governments resisted.) Finally, the years 1968 and 1969 witnessed a fairly steep rise of international interest rates. (The federal funds rate in the United States climbed from 4.22% in 1967 to 8.21% in 1969.) This was transmitted from the United States to Europe via the Eurodollar market, which patently revealed to European countries the increasing restraints which the internationalization of capital markets put on their capacity to pursue autonomous monetary policies.

The speculation against the French franc and in favour of the German mark was revived in the wake of President de Gaulle's resignation in April 1969. On 8 August, the new French Government devalued the franc by 11.1%, and for the first time 'monetary compensatory amounts' (MCAs) were introduced to avoid having to increase agricultural prices by the same percentage on the French internal market.

It was thus decided to maintain farm prices in francs at their previous level, on condition that France should gradually increase her internal agricultural prices until they reach the European level. Meanwhile a complex system of differentiated taxes applying to agricultural products when crossing the French border was set up. French agricultural products were subjected to an export tax equal to the devaluation, and agricultural products imported by France received an equivalent subsidy. These 'monetary compensatory amounts' were designed to offset the effects of the exchange rate changes while preserving the CAP's principles.

After a short period of floating, the German mark was revalued by 9.3% on 24 October 1969. Again, but in the opposite direction to France's, a system of MCAs was put into place. Neither the decision to devalue the franc nor the one to let the mark float were the subject of preliminary consultations, the Council's 1964 decision notwithstanding. Whatever illusion could remain over the *de facto* existence of monetary union was shattered in the wake of those parity changes and of the lack of coordination which surrounded them.

These internal developments of the Community, occurring at a time when the international monetary environment had become increasingly threatening and signs of disintegration of the Bretton Woods system were multiplying, were probably sufficient to overcome a natural caution, and to persuade European leaders that negative integration had to be complemented by more positive steps leading to common policies and a true economic and monetary union.

3. From the proposal for an economic and monetary union to the creation of the European Monetary System

(*a*) At the European Summit of The Hague on 1 and 2 December 1969, the German Chancellor Willy Brandt launched the proposal for an economic and monetary union and proposed two stages towards that end. The first stage would seek to harmonize short-term economic policies and to define medium-term quantitative objectives. The second stage would see the establishment of a European reserve fund to which member countries would transfer part of their foreign exchange reserves. Chancellor Brandt's European partners accepted these ideas and during the following months the Council undertook the task of putting flesh on the bones of The Hague agreement.

In January 1970 the Council adopted most of the proposals contained in the first Barre plan, except the mechanism of medium-term financial assistance. The system of short-term monetary support formally came into effect on 9 February 1970 following a decision by the Committee of the Governors of the Central Banks.

In February, a meeting of the finance ministers revealed the existence of a fairly broad agreement over ultimate objectives and over a maximum duration of 10 years for the transitional stage leading to economic and monetary union. But, on the substance of the reforms to be introduced during the transitional stage, there remained important differences of opinion. A *working party* chaired by Mr *Werner* was charged with preparing a report on these differences and on the means to overcome them.

The dissension which arose in this group reflected the differences which had already arisen at the meeting of finance ministers and between Chancellor Brandt and President Pompidou at the summit of The Hague. At stake was an age-old conflict we mentioned earlier (p. 32).

On the one side, the 'economists', represented chiefly by the Germans and the Dutch, put the coordination of economic policies first, as they considered it an indispensable preliminary to deeper monetary coordination. According to this view, monetary union would be the crowning achievement of a gradual process that would first harmonize and then unify economic policies.

On the other side, the 'monetarist' faction, consisting of the Belgians, the French and the Luxembourgers, upheld the thesis according to which rapid progress in the monetary field would be the surest way of compelling governments to coordinate their economic policies more effectively.

In the provisional report which the Werner group submitted to the finance ministers in June 1970, the 'monetarists' specifically proposed to narrow the fluctuation margins between European currencies and to set up an exchange stabilization fund in the first stage. Needless to say, the 'economists' could not agree with these proposals.

(b) The 'monetarists' wish to narrow fluctuation margins between EEC currencies was based on a twofold preoccupation:

(i)   first, to the extent that the ultimate goal was a perfect fixity of exchange rates, or even a single currency, it seemed fitting to progress in that direction by gradually narrowing the authorized fluctuation margin;

(ii) moreover, in the system prevailing at the time, the fluctuation margin between any two currencies other than the dollar was twice the margin between either one of these currencies and the dollar. The official parities of European currencies were determined in relation to gold, and therefore also in relation to the dollar, which was officially convertible into gold at the fixed rate of USD 35 to the ounce. Each country that was a party to the 1958 European monetary agreement was authorized to vary the parity of its currency by a maximum of 0.75% on either side of its dollar parity. If at a given time country A's currency stood at its ceiling against the dollar while country B's was at its floor, currency A could at most decline by 1.5% against the dollar, while currency B could at most move up by 1.5% against the dollar. This implied thus that currency A could at most move down by 3% *against currency B,* which event would occur if currency A moved from its ceiling to its floor while at the same time currency B made the opposite move. From this effect, rooted in the logical structure of the gold-exchange standard, followed *inter alia* the consequence that the dollar had greater liquidity than other currencies, since the exchange risk carried by holding a currency in a central bank's or in a private portfolio was twice as small for the dollar.

In order to narrow the fluctuation margin between European currencies while preserving the dollar's central role in the system, a machinery of joint fluctuation by European currencies against the dollar had to be devised—a 'snake' inside the 'tunnel' formed by their fluctuation margins *vis-à-vis* the dollar. The diameter of the tunnel was determined by the fluctuation margin around the dollar parity, that is 1.5%. The width of the snake would be given by the intra-Community margin, smaller than 1.5%, around the central rate defining the parity of a European currency relative to another one. This central rate would be allowed to move up and down against the dollar parity, thus around the axis of the tunnel—and the more so as the intra-Community margin would be narrower than the tunnel—but in such a way that the snake would always be kept inside the tunnel. [4]

---

[4] The operation of this type of machinery is illustrated in a clear and detailed fashion, using figures and diagrams, in the article by A.E. Nivollet, 'Le serpent monétaire européen', in *Les Cahiers Français,* No 196, May-June 1980.

Narrowing the fluctuation margins between European currencies was supposed to produce the following results:

(i) It would decrease the exchange risk attached to holding European currencies relative to the dollar, and thus would increase their attractiveness as reserve assets for European central banks.

(ii) It would compel these central banks to intervene more frequently in order to observe the intra-Community margins, but to a greater extent than before one would be able to use Community currencies for such interventions. The 'stabilization fund' which the 'monetarists' recommended would make it easier to narrow the margins and to use Community currencies for interventions.

(iii) It would reduce the degree of independence of monetary policies among Member States and this, according to the 'monetarists', would promote a more effective harmonization of those policies.

(iv) Finally, the joint fluctuation of European currencies *vis-à-vis* the dollar would emphasize the Community's 'monetary personality' against the rest of the world, and would thus be a first step leading to a common monetary policy toward foreign countries.

It goes without saying that, to the eyes of the 'economists', all these consequences of monetary integration seemed premature in the absence of a preliminary harmonization of economic policies.

(*c*) In its final version, which was submitted to the Council and to the Commission on 8 October 1970, the *Werner report* presents a compromise between the views of the 'economists' and the 'monetarists'. The principle of parallel progress toward the convergence of economic policies and toward monetary integration was clearly stated.

In respect to the coordination of economic policies, the report contained a number of suggestions bearing on fiscal policy, the financing of deficits, tax policies and financial markets. In the monetary field, the report underlined the need for Member States to harmonize their monetary policy instruments and to experiment, in the first stage, with a narrowing of fluctuation margins between their currencies, the ultimate objective remaining to ensure a complete freedom of capital movements and a total convertibility of their currencies at rates that would be irrevocably fixed.

A European Monetary Cooperation Fund was to be set up, at the latest during the second stage, in order to manage the machinery of short-term monetary support (which was set up in a January 1970 decision by the Council). It was also to provide medium-term financial assistance, and would be progressively entrusted with the management of the Community's foreign exchange reserves.

In the wake of the publication of the Werner report, it appeared that disagreements remained among Member States over the final stage of the process of economic and monetary integration, particularly because an important part of French public opinion was not prepared to accept the loss of national sovereignty which it seemingly entailed. Nevertheless, the *Council, on 22 March 1971,* was able to reach an agreement by adopting a resolution on the achievement by stages of economic and monetary union in the Community, and by specifying the principles of action for a first stage of three years.

Among these principles were the setting up of a mechanism for medium-term financial assistance and the gradual narrowing of fluctuation margins among European currencies, starting on 1 June 1971.

But no later than May the international monetary crisis intensified and thwarted the application of this second principle. Growing speculation against the dollar put strong upward pressures on the German mark. The Bonn Government proposed that European currencies should jointly float against the dollar, but neither France nor Italy could accept this idea. On 10 May 1971, the mark and the guilder started floating while controls of capital movements were introduced in other Community countries to try to contain speculation.

On 15 August 1971, President Nixon announced the US Government's decision to suspend officially the gold convertibility of the dollar. Other countries were thus released from their obligation to maintain the dollar parity of their currency within conventional margins.

In the face of this change in the rules of the game, Europe's monetary disunion was blatantly revealed. At the Council of 19 August 1971, the Benelux countries proposed to keep the fluctuations of Community currencies within previous margins and to float jointly against the dollar, but failed to persuade their partners. They chose therefore to adopt this system for themselves, and this became in fact the very first version of the 'snake', though limited to the three countries of Benelux. Germany continued to let her currency freely float and was imitated by Italy. Finally France set up a double exchange market and strengthened exchange controls.

(*d*) With the intention of restoring some order in the international monetary system, the ministers of the 'Group of Ten' met at the *Smithsonian Institute* in Washington on 17 and 18 December 1971. The agreement they reached at that meeting determined a new parity grid for the principal currencies in relation to the dollar, which itself was devalued by 7.9% in relation to gold. Relative to the dollar, the mark was revalued by 13.5%, the Belgian franc and the guilder by 11.6%, the French franc and the pound sterling by 8.6%, and the lira by 7.5%.

The Smithsonian agreement provided further that fluctuation margins for other currencies against the dollar would be widened to 2.25% on either side of the new dollar parities. The diameter of the tunnel in which European currencies could move was thus multiplied by three, going from 1.5% to 4.5%, with the consequence that the maximum spread between any two of these currencies could now reach 4.5% at a given moment and 9% over a certain period (during which one of the two currencies would move from its ceiling to its floor against the dollar while simultaneously the other currency would make the opposite move).

Fluctuations of such amplitude could well have jeopardized the common agricultural policy. Besides, following the suspension of the dollar convertibility in August 1971 and its devaluation a few months later, mistrust of the dollar became general. All the European central banks were now anxious to avoid accumulating dollar balances and ready to reinforce European solidarity to that end.

41

Internal as well as external considerations were thus leading towards new attempts at European monetary integration, the outcome of which were the Council's decisions of February and March 1972 and the Basle Agreement of 10 April between the central banks of the six member countries. The 'snake in the tunnel' was thus born.

According to the Basle Agreement, the spot spread between the parities of any two EEC currencies could not be greater than 2.25%, which was the authorized margin between any one of these currencies and the dollar. Moreover the August 1971 decision on the Benelux currencies was still in force, and in consequence the authorized maximum spread between the guilder and the Belgian franc was 1.5%. The width of the snake (2.25%) was thus half the width of the tunnel (4.5%). In addition, it was agreed in principle that intervention aimed at keeping European currencies inside the snake would use European currencies, while intervention in dollars would only be allowed to prevent the snake from leaving the tunnel. This provision answered both a request by Germany, anxious not to have to accumulate too many dollar balances while intervening in support of other European currencies, and France's wish to reduce, partly for political reasons, the role of the dollar as a reserve currency.

On 1 May the pound sterling, the Irish pound and the Danish krone joined the snake. The procedure for these three countries' admission to the EEC was then under way and was to be concluded with their entry into the Community on 1 January 1973.

However, sterling was rapidly swept away by the continuous wave of speculation against the dollar, and on 23 June it left the snake as well as the tunnel, accompanied by the Irish pound. The Danish krone left the snake on 27 June but joined it again on 10 October.

Such events undoubtedly showed that, in an increasingly volatile international environment, the system put into place by the Basle Agreement remained fragile. A solemn restatement of their monetary cohesiveness seemed necessary to some of the European partners. The Summit of Paris in October 1972 reaffirmed the will of the European Community Member States to press ahead toward the irreversible achievement of an economic and monetary union. This statement of intentions was not, however, followed with concrete results, save for the creation of a *European Monetary Cooperation Fund* (EMCF) [5] which had been decided by the finance ministers in September 1972 and was ratified by the Paris Summit.

(*e*) Switzerland's decision to let her currency float in January 1973 was the signal of a new attack against the dollar. On 13 February the dollar was devalued again while the Italian lira left the snake. Besides, the US authorities let it be known they would no longer intervene in support of the dollar on the foreign exchange market.

The EEC Commission then proposed a system of joint floating of the European currencies against the dollar, thus preserving the snake but letting it out of the tunnel. This would include the possibility, within limits and under certain conditions, of modifying parities within the snake. This new element of flexibility, which foreshadows the EMS

---

[5] Translator's note: The EMCF is better known by its French acronym FECOM (*Fonds européen de coopération monétaire*), which will be used in the rest of the book.

'stable but adjustable' parities, was proposed with the intention *inter alia* of bringing the pound and the lira back into the snake. However, no agreement by the Nine (the United Kingdom, Ireland and Denmark being members of the EEC since 1 January) could be concluded on the basis of these proposals. On 12 March 1973, six countries—Germany, France, Denmark, and the Benelux countries—decided to let their currencies float jointly, with the mark being revalued by 3%. The pound sterling, the Irish pound and the Italian lira continued to float independently.

These decisions served notice of the abolition of the tunnel, but at the same time pointed to the desire of the six snake partners to stabilize exchange rates among themselves, in a world where exchange rate flexibility had become the general rule. This 'islet of stability' proved attractive to Norway and Sweden, whose currencies joined the snake on 14 March 1973.

Nevertheless such stability was only relative, both in view of much coming and going in the snake and because parity changes were fairly frequent. The advent of the first oil shock at the end of 1973 and the extensive difficulties it provoked in regard to both inflation and the balance of payments evidently contributed to this state of affairs.

Thus the French franc left the snake on 19 January 1974, rejoined it on 10 July 1975, and left it again on 15 March 1976. The Swedish krona left the snake on 28 August 1977 and the Norwegian krone on 12 December 1978. As early as January 1974, out of the nine EEC Member States, only Germany, Denmark and the Benelux countries remained in the snake. For the latter group of countries, the August 1971 special agreement limiting the spread between rates to 1.5% was suspended in March 1976.

As to the parity changes which occurred within the snake, there is a long list:

12 March 1973:	3% revaluation of the mark;
29 June 1973:	5.5% revaluation of the mark;
17 September 1973:	5% revaluation of the guilder;
16 November 1973:	5% revaluation of the Norwegian krone;
17 October 1976:	'Frankfurt realignment':
	– the mark is revalued by 2%,
	– the Danish krone is devalued by 4%,
	– the Norwegian and Swedish currencies are devalued by 1%;
1 April 1977:	6% devaluation of the Swedish krona;
	3% devaluation of the Danish and Norwegian kroner;
28 August 1977:	5% devaluation of the Danish and Norwegian kroner (the Swedish krona leaves the snake);
13 February 1978:	8% devaluation of the Norwegian krone;
17 October 1978:	4% revaluation of the mark;
	2% revaluation of the guilder and the Belgian franc.

(*f*) Compared with the ambitions expressed at the summits of The Hague in 1969 and of Paris in 1972, the progress toward economic and monetary union amounted to little over the period 1973-77. While it succeeded in maintaining a certain monetary stability inside a zone centred on the German mark, the 'snake out of the tunnel' suffered many vicissitudes. But it is doubtful whether one could have hoped for more, in a world shaken by the divergence of inflation rates and of balance-of-payments difficulties which industrialized countries experienced following the first oil shock.

Moreover, within the European Community, this divergence in economic performance and in the reactions to the first oil shock clearly showed that the coordination of economic policies, which according to the Werner report was due to accompany monetary integration, was in fact far from satisfactory. To be sure, some coordination took place both within the Council and in the various committees established in 1964, but it retained a consultative character and seldom produced precise policies.

During this period, the lack of monetary integration which manifested itself in the *de facto* division of the Community in several indifferently coordinated monetary zones, could well have jeopardized the smooth operation of the agricultural common market while increasingly fostering protectionist temptations. A 'cumulative logic of disintegration' was dangerously creeping forward.

Various proposals were made to counter these pernicious tendencies. At the end of 1973, the Commission proposed reinforcing the convergence of economic policies. It was followed by the Council with its February 1974 decision on 'the pursuit of a higher degree of convergence of economic policies'.

In September 1974 Mr *Fourcade,* the French Minister for Finance, proposed a plan of 'concerted floating' of all the Community currencies, which aimed at tightening the coordination between the five currencies of the snake and the four currencies that independently floated. He proposed to start from the snake as it existed, but to form around it a kind of 'boa', wider and more pliable, which would include the European currencies outside the snake. This envelope around the snake could have margins wider than the snake's, and allow for the possible exit and re-entry of currencies.

The Fourcade plan also provided for joint interventions by Community countries on the foreign exchange market in order to keep the dollar at its 'Community level'. Lastly it contained suggestions on the enlargement of Community credit facilities and on the definition of a new unit of account. In May 1975 Mr Fourcade proposed in addition that the responsibility for intervention should not fall only on the central bank whose currency was at the bottom of the intra-Community margin. These proposals met with a fairly cold reception, but their echo can be found in some of the EMS provisions as well as in current debates.

In December 1975 the Belgian Prime Minister Mr *Leo Tindemans,* in his report on the European Union, developed a series of proposals aimed at strengthening the snake, giving it a more Community-like character and broadening its action to cover the key elements of economic and monetary policy. According to Mr Tindemans, a strengthening of the snake was also likely to facilitate the progressive return to more international monetary stability. The first stage would consist of creating throughout the world large zones of stability within which stable exchange rates would be maintained.

In February 1976, the Dutch Finance Minister Mr *Duisenberg,* who chaired the Council of Ministers of the economy and for finance in the Community, proposed to bring European currencies closer and to improve the coordination of economic policies by the creation of 'target zones'. These would not be constraining and would be defined in terms of effective exchange rates, for the floating currencies and for the snake as an entity. A currency leaving its target zone would, according to this proposal, set in motion a procedure of consultations with the Commission and the partner countries.

These various proposals, which showed the existence of a current of opinion still in favour of European monetary integration, reached their climax in a resounding speech delivered in *Florence* on 27 October 1977 by the President of the Commission Mr *Roy Jenkins.* Monetary union—and the stability that would result therefrom—was proposed as the best way to promote a recovery of growth and to reinforce the fight against inflation and unemployment.

In addition, in February and March 1978, we proposed to bring European currencies nearer to each other in the following ways: [6] the snake would be maintained as it existed, and the other European currencies not belonging to the snake would be encompassed in a single target zone which would be demarcated by the weighted average of the fluctuations of the snake and of the dollar, with equal weights at the outset. This target zone for floating currencies was to gradually evolve toward the snake as the weight of the latter would be gradually increased.

The target zone was to be used initially as a threshold, setting in motion a consultation procedure at the Community level whenever the market rates moved away from the target zone. The system we proposed also comprised an obligation of negative intervention, in the form of a commitment to avoid policy measures that would bring the exchange rate under its target zone.

The proposal contained in addition a component of coordination of domestic economic and monetary policies and provided for a strengthening of the Community credit mechanisms to allow for a greater use of Community currencies rather than dollars for intervention.

Finally, it was suggested that for the settlement of such Community credits one could partly use a common European currency whose unit would be the European unit of account, that is a basket of Community currencies. This European currency would be issued by the European Monetary Cooperation Fund and would be partly secured by the member countries' gold deposits. This would be a concrete way to mobilize in part the central banks' gold reserves. But to protect the Community countries from the accusation of fixing an official price of gold, it was proposed that the European currency would be issued to the amount of 80% of the value of the gold security, appraised at the market rate. For credits granted in a European currency, the rate of interest would be a weighted average of the current interest rates in the Community countries.

Thus the EMS could blossom on ground that was made relatively fertile by previous proposals.

On 7 April 1978, at the European Council of Copenhagen, Chancellor Schmidt and President Giscard d'Estaing launched the idea of a new European Monetary System in which all the Community countries would participate. Three months later, the European Council of Bremen gave its official seal of approval to the German-French initiative and instructed the Ministers for Finance to elaborate a system based on a European currency unit (the ECU), provided with rules as strict as the snake's, and endowed with substantial financial means by the pooling of part of the reserves. The conditions of operation of the EMS were adopted by the European Council of Brussels on 5 and 6 December 1978. [7]

---

[6] See J. van Ypersele: 'Rapprocher les monnaies européennes', *Trends*, February and April 1978.
[7] Peter Ludlow's work (op. cit) is particularly well documented over this last pre-EMS period, especially the year 1978.

Chapter III —
The EMS and the conditions
for its proper operation

1. The novelty of the EMS compared with the snake

To some observers the European Monetary System may appear as little more than an expanded and rechristened snake. Indeed, as in the snake, membership in the EMS is optional. While France, Italy and Ireland chose to adhere to it side by side with former snake members (that is, Germany, Denmark and the Benelux countries), the United Kingdom decided in 1978 to stay free from the EMS exchange rate mechanism, which is its essential component. A consequence of this was the breaking of the long-standing parity between the Irish pound and sterling. Likewise, when Greece joined the European Community in 1981, she chose not to participate in the EMS. At the present time, eight Member States of the European Community thus adhere to the EMS exchange rate mechanism.

The duties flowing from this adhesion are also very similar to those that existed in the snake. A currency cannot vary relative to another by more than 2.25% around their bilateral parity (for the Italian lira however this margin is 6% at present). Whenever an EMS currency reaches the limit of its authorized margin *vis-à-vis* another currency, the two concerned central banks must intervene to prevent the crossing of this boundary. Of course this symmetry is a fairly formal matter, for the burden of intervention is clearly heavier for the weak-currency country, forced to draw on its reserves, than for the strong-currency country, which confines itself to injecting additional liquidity into its economy.

Besides these similarities there exist however important differences: they essentially bear on the *role of the ECU,* on the mechanism of the *divergence indicator,* and on the transition to the *institutional phase* of the EMS, which was foreseen at the time of its creation.

— The ECU (the name of which echoes an ancient French currency while also being an acronym for European currency unit) is first and foremost a composite monetary unit, similar in its composition to the older European monetary unit of account (EMUA) and consisting of a basket of definite amounts of each Community currency. Sterling, though not participating in the exchange rate mechanism, belonged from the start to the ECU basket. The Greek drachma joined it on the occasion of the revision of the basket, which occurred on 15 September 1984. This revision will be commented upon below, and the precise composition of the ECU will then be given.

But the ECU is not simply an accounting unit, and it has been assigned a more important role than the EMUA it has replaced. For the exchange rate mechanism naturally includes, for participating central banks, an obligation to intervene on the foreign exchange market whenever a currency is in danger of crossing its limit of fluctuation relative to another. This obligation implies the existence of *credit mechanisms* that will supply, as it were, the ammunition with which the central banks will perform their duties and defend the parities. To these credit mechanisms are attached *rules for settlement* and an *instrument of settlement*: at this juncture, as we shall see, we find again the ECU, which in the EMS serves as a means of settlement between the European Community central banks and as a reserve asset.

The rate of the ECU in terms of any Community currency is equal to the sum of the equivalents in that currency of the amounts of all the currencies contained in the ECU basket. According to whether, for these equivalents, one takes the bilateral central rate of each currency or its market rate (which can deviate from the central rate within the limits of the authorized fluctuation margin), he shall obtain the central rate of the ECU in terms of that currency, or its market value.

— The spread between those two ECU rates is the basis for calculating the divergence *indicator,* which is another novelty of the EMS compared to the snake. This mechanism was introduced into the EMS as a result of a compromise. [1]

The Bremen Agreement did not specify how the obligation to intervene on the foreign exchange market was to be defined. Long discussions took place over the question whether it would be defined in relation to the ECU or whether the system of the parity grid as it existed in the snake would still be used.

The supporters of a system based upon the ECU wanted the intervention obligation to be defined in relation to the average of European currencies and to be called forth, for a specific currency, as soon as the maximum authorized deviation between the central rate and the market value of the ECU in terms of that currency was reached. The burden of intervention and of adjustment would thus fall upon the currency that would diverge from this average, whether the divergence be upward or downward. Thus they deemed that such a system would have greater symmetry in its obligations, since they would fall not only on the diverging weak currency but equally on the diverging strong currency.

By contrast, the supporters of a system based on the parity grid [2] upheld the definition, as in the snake, of bilateral intervention limits for each of the system's currencies relative to the others. They mostly stressed the technical complexity of using the ECU to define

---

[1] See J. van Ypersele, 'Le nouveau système monétaire européen' in *Bulletin de Documentation* du Service d'Études et de Documentation du Ministère des Finances, No 4, April 1979.

[2] See (among others) Niels Thygesen: *A European Monetary System. The major issues after Bremen.* International Centre for Monetary and Banking Studies, Geneva, September 1978.

intervention limits. They pointed out in particular that such a system would operate with great difficulty if the exchange rate mechanism did not include all the currencies: a currency like sterling, which although floating enters nevertheless into the composition of the ECU basket, could influence its value and thus be the cause of divergence for the currencies participating in the exchange rate mechanism.

Moreover, they emphasized the fact that small currencies, whose weight in the ECU is limited, would be subject to compulsory intervention more frequently and more importantly than large currencies. The greater the weight of a currency in the ECU basket, the less the market value of the ECU in terms of that currency will be influenced by movements of the other currencies. Finally they argued that, in a system based on the ECU, the divergence of a currency in one direction would not necessarily be accompanied by the divergence of another currency in the opposite direction, and that this would make it difficult to determine without additional rules which currency should be used for intervention.

Besides these technical objections, the opponents of an ECU-based system raised a more fundamental objection. They feared that the greater symmetry implied by such a system would have inflationary consequences, since it allowed for the possibility that a strong currency could diverge owing to the simple fact that the combined weight of weak currencies might become dominant in the basket. Thus the strong-currency country could well reach its divergence limit and be forced to intervene, at the risk of having to accept in consequence an acceleration of its own inflation, before the weak-currency countries had reached their own divergence limits.

Finally, after lengthy debates, the European partners rallied to the formula, worked out in the technical discussions, of the so-called 'Belgian compromise'. This formula amounted to retaining an exchange rate mechanism and intervention obligations based upon the bilateral parity grid, but superimposing on it a mechanism based upon the deviation of a currency from the average of the other currencies, that is, the ECU-based *divergence indicator*. This second mechanism, however, unlike the first, did not include an obligation to intervene, but only a presumption to take action. (This 'presumption of action' represents in fact a second compromise between those for whom crossing the divergence threshold should activate the obligation to intervene, and those for whom it was only to set a consultation procedure in motion.) Later on we shall analyse in detail the operation of this mechanism.

— In one final respect, the proponents of the EMS hoped that it would be more than an exchange rate mechanism or an improved version of the snake. Its future consolidation, by way of a transition to what was called *'the institutional phase'*, was expressly foreseen from the outset. On this point we cannot do better than to quote the resolution of the European Council of 5 December 1978: 'We remain firmly resolved to consolidate, not later than two years after the start of the scheme, into a final system the provisions and procedures thus created. This system will entail the creation of the European Monetary Fund as announced in the conclusions of the European Council meeting at Bremen on 6 and 7 July 1978, as well as the full utilization of the ECU as a reserve asset and a means of settlement. It will be based on adequate legislation at the Community as well as the national level'.

However, as we shall see in Chapter V, this calendar could not be observed. At present the EMS mechanisms are still those that were put into place in 1978.

In the rest of this chapter, we would like to explain those mechanisms, first by examining in succession the *exchange rate mechanism,* the *role of the ECU* and the *credit mechanism,* and then by analysing in the abstract the conditions for the proper functioning of these mechanisms, taking into particular account the objections against the EMS at the time of its creation. The next chapter, by retracing the EMS experience to date, will allow a more empirical examination of the manner in which it has performed so far. [3]

2. The exchange rate and intervention mechanism [4]

As we have just seen, this mechanism contains two components:

(i)   One is based on the maintenance of bilateral parities or, as they are called, bilateral central rates between participating currencies. Around these central rates bilateral limits of fluctuation must be enforced by way of compulsory and unlimited intervention on the foreign exchange market.

(ii) The other is based on the divergence indicator, the purpose of which is to establish a presumption of action on the part of the authorities in charge of the currency whose rate would exceed certain limits fixed in terms of the ECU.

(a) Central rates and rules for intervention

All the EEC currencies (including the drachma since 17 September 1984) have an *ECU-related central rate.* The pound sterling (like the drachma) is not participating in the exchange rate mechanism, but for the sake of the operation of the divergence indicator (see (*b*) below) it has been assigned a notional central rate. This notional central rate can be modified on the occasion of each parity realignment in the EMS, if at the time the market rate of the pound sterling is outside the band of ±2.25% around its notional central rate. [5] The same arrangement now applies to the drachma.

---

[3] The whole of the texts relating to the European Monetary System, texts which abrogate or replace, as of 13.3.1979, the former provisions concerning the snake, are set out in Annex 2.

[4] In writing this and the following sections, we drew in part on the excellent study of 'The European Monetary System' in the July 1979 issue of *European Economy,* published by the Commission of the European Communities, Directorate-General for Economic and Financial Affairs.

[5] Thus, on the occasion of the latest (21 March 1983) realignment, the ECU-related notional central rate of the pound sterling was devalued by 11.2% on the basis of its market rate of the day before. Twice since however, sterling's notional central rate has served as an 'adjustment variable' and was modified outside of a parity realignment.

First, on 17 May 1983, the Council determined a new notional central rate, based on the market rate of 13 May, up 7.3% from the rate fixed on 21 March, and this in order to ease the settlement of the agricultural problem. This decision resulted in a new set of ECU related central rates for all the other EMS currencies, but the bilateral central rates and the intervention limits remained unchanged.

A second time, during the revision of the ECU basket on 15 September 1984, the Council modified the notional central rate of the pound sterling in such a way that the revision did not affect the ECU-related central rates for the currencies participating in the exchange rate mechanism—which therefore kept their values fixed on 17 May 1983—nor the bilateral parities, which remained at their respective levels of 21 March 1983.

TABLE III - 1

Parities and intervention points of EMS currencies (applicable from 21 March 1983)

		Amsterdam in HFL	Brussels in BFR/LFR	Frankfurt in DM	Copenhagen in DKR	London in UKL	Dublin in IRL	Paris in FF	Rome in LIT
HFL 100	+2.25%		1 818.0	90.770	329.63		29.3832	278.35	58 997.0
	central rate	100	1 777.58	88.7526	322.297	[1]	28.7295	272.158	55 563.0
	−2.25%		1 738.0	86.780	315.13		28.0904	266.10	52 329.0
BFR/LFR 100	+2.25%	5.7535		5.106	18.543		1.6530	15.659	3 318.9
	central rate	5.62561	100	4.99288	18.1312	[1]	1.61621	15.3106	3 125.76
	−2.25%	5.5005		4.882	17.727		1.5803	14.97	2 943.8
DM 100	+2.25%	115.235	2 048.35		371.40		33.1015	313.63	66 473.0
	central rate	112.673	2 002.85	100	363.141	[1]	32.3703	306.648	62 604.3
	−2.25%	110.1675	1 958.50		355.06		31.6455	299.85	58 960.0
DKR 100	+2.25%	31.7325	564.10	28.165			9.1168	86.365	18 305.0
	central rate	31.0273	551.536	27.5375	100	[1]	8.91396	84.4432	17 239.7
	−2.25%	30.3375	539.30	26.925			8.7157	82.565	16 236.0
UKL 1	central rate	[1]	[1]	[1]	[1]	[1]	[1]	[1]	—
IRL 1	+2.25%	3.5600	63.2810	3.160	11.4735			9.6885	2 053.53
	central rate	3.48075	61.8732	3.08925	11.2184	[1]	1	9.47313	1 934.01
	−2.25%	3.4030	60.4965	3.021	10.9687			9.2625	1 821.45
FF 100	+2.25%	37.58	668.00	33.350	121.11		10.7964		21 677.0
	central rate	36.7434	653.144	32.6107	118.423	[1]	10.5562	100	20 415.7
	−2.25%	35.925	638.60	31.885	115.78		10.3214		19 227.0
LIT 1 000	+6%	1.911	33.970	1.696	6.159		0.549015	5.201	
	central rate	1.79976	31.9922	1.59733	5.80057		0.517061	4.89819	1 000.0
	−6%	1.69500	30.130	1.504	5.463		0.486968	4.6130	
ECU 1	central rate	2.52595	44.9008	2.24184	8.14104	(0.585992)	0.72569	6.87456	1 403.49

[1] Does not participate in the exchange rate mechanism.

The ECU-related central rates are expressed as a certain quantity of currency per ECU, as indicated in the last line of the following table. (Thus, more properly speaking, it is a central rate of the ECU in terms of currency X rather than a central rate of currency X in terms of the ECU.) By linking together the ECU-related central rates we obtain for each currency participating in the EMS a series of *bilateral central rates,* the juxtaposition of which constitutes the parity grid. Central rates can be changed by common consent, following a procedure in which all the countries participating in the exchange rate mechanism are involved, along with the Commission. Table III-1 presents the parity grid as it resulted from the realignment on 21 March 1983 as well as the series of ECU-related central rates born of the 17 May decision and, for sterling's notional rate, of the 15 September 1984 decision.

Around these bilateral central rates, margins of authorized fluctuation stretch to $\pm 2.25\%$ and are bounded, for each currency *vis-à-vis* another, by its *intervention limits.* However, Member States whose currencies did not belong to the snake in December 1978 (which was the case for France, Ireland and Italy) were given the right to opt for wider margins of up to 6%. Italy has availed itself of this opportunity. This wider margin is intended to be gradually reduced as soon as economic conditions permit.

Intervention is compulsory whenever a currency reaches its intervention limit relative to another. The issuing banks of the two currencies are then required to intervene on their respective markets in order to keep these currencies within their fluctuation margins. In other words, the issuing bank of the strong currency purchases the weak currency on its foreign exchange market, while the issuing bank of the weak currency sells the strong currency (if necessary by first borrowing it from the issuing central bank).

As a matter of fact, observance of the limits is to some extent guaranteed by the market itself, which 'comes' to the central bank whenever a limit is reached, since no party will deal in a foreign currency at a less advantageous rate than the one he knows he can obtain from the monetary authorities. Under those circumstances the latter are obliged to meet the market demand for the currency. This is the reason why the obligation to intervene in Community currencies at the intervention limits is, in theory, unlimited.

Apart from compulsory intervention at the bilateral limits, the system also makes provision for intervention before these limits are reached. There are basically two types of such *intra-marginal intervention.*

There exist, firstly, optional operations that are initiated by central banks. Such interventions are generally operated in order to cut short the tendency of a currency to draw near its limit, failing which the compulsory interventions that would take place at the limit might well require more substantial amounts. In most cases so far these interventions have been in dollars, for the plain reason that, in order to use a partner's currency inside the margins, participants need his permission, which is not the case for using dollars. In the EMS this may pose an embarassing problem both at the Community level and at the international level, for if such intervention becomes too frequent it would tend to clash with the principle of intervention in Community currencies, as laid down by the European Council (see Resolution of 5 December 1978 in Annex 2).

It should be underlined here that in case of dollar interventions, the credit mechanisms available within the FECOM (European Monetary Cooperation Fund) and described below are not applicable, and that too frequent an eclipse of these mechanisms might well jeopardize one of the principal functions of the ECU.

The second type of intra-marginal intervention is a novelty. It consists of the intra-marginal intervention that a country may have to perform under the rules governing the operation of the divergence indicator, which will be dealt with now.

(b) The divergence indicator

One of the new elements of the EMS that makes it different from the snake, which was based only on the parity grid, is the divergence indicator. This device makes it possible to locate the position and the movement of an EMS currency relative to the Community average represented by the ECU.

To do so, one calculates first the *maximum divergence spread* for each currency. This spread represents the maximum percentage appreciation or depreciation which the market rate of the ECU in terms of a given currency may show against its central rate. It will be reached when the rate of this currency deviates by 2.25% in the same direction from all the other EMS currencies.

One might think for a moment that this maximum divergence spread is itself equal to 2.25% but this is not the case. For the currency whose maximum divergence spread is being computed itself accounts for a certain proportion of the ECU. Therefore, even when this currency deviates by 2.25% from all the others, its own weight in the ECU automatically gives a certain inertia to the market rate of the ECU expressed in that currency, and the latter rate can only deviate from its central rate by a percentage which is necessarily inferior to 2.25%. Thus the maximum divergence spread will not be the same for all currencies: it will in fact be the higher — and closer to 2.25% — the smaller the weight of the currency in the ECU basket; its value is thus 2.22 for the Irish pound and 1.53 for the mark.

Evidently, the special 6% fluctuation margins which Italy opted for also apply to the calculation of the maximum divergence spread for the lira, which is 5.40.

The *divergence indicator* shows the extent to which a given currency is nearing its maximum spread. This is done by relating the premium or the discount, in the market rate of the ECU in terms of that currency, to the above-mentioned maximum spread. This ratio, expressed in percent, is the divergence indicator. When it reaches 75%, the implicated currency is said to be at its *divergence threshold*.

There exists however an additional cause of complexity. As the maximum divergence spread, for currencies other than the lira, is calculated under the assumption that bilateral fluctuations are $\pm 2.25\%$, a corrective mechanism is needed to prevent the indicator of currencies with a narrow fluctuation margin from being distorted by exchange rate movements of the currencies which either have a wide fluctuation margin (lira) or do not participate in the exchange rate mechanism (sterling). This corrective mechanism thus aims at neutralizing the effect on the divergence indicator of fluctuations in sterling or the lira which overstep the supposedly uniform margin of 2.25%: the correction consists of deducting from the movement of appreciation or depreciation shown by the market rate of the ECU the share of this movement which can be ascribed to the overstepping of the 2.25% bilateral margin by the lira or the pound sterling.

However this correction, made necessary by the relative anomaly which the peculiar situations of sterling and of the lira constitute in the EMS, is only a second-best which can itself entail other drawbacks. Thus, whenever one of these two currencies moves beyond the 2.25% spread relative to a third currency, the latter's divergence indicator, *ceteris paribus*, will not move. This corrective mechanism thus gives the indicator a certain inertia, and for instance the persisting strength of sterling in 1980 partially accounts for the fact that one of the weak currencies of the system at the time, namely the Belgian franc, remained for a fairly long period beyond its divergence threshold. [6]

We shall now illustrate how the divergence indicator is calculated in practice. Let us see, for instance for the Belgian franc, first what the ECU-related central rate is, and then what the intervention point is when all the other EEC currencies simultaneously show an appreciation or depreciation of 2.25% against the Belgian franc (see Table III-2).

TABLE III-2

Parity and intervention point of the ECU in terms of the Belgian franc since 17 September 1984
(figures rounded off)

Composition of the ECU		Equivalent, in BFR, of the components of the ECU where	
		(a) Each EEC currency is at par with the BFR	(b) Each EEC currency shows a depreciation of 2.25% against the BFR
		BFR	BFR
BFR ⎫ LFR ⎬	3.850	3.85	3.85
HFL	0.256	4.55	4.45
DKR	0.219	1.21	1.18
DM	0.719	14.40	14.08
LIT	140.000	4.48	4.38
FF	1.310	8.56	8.37
UKL	0.0878	6.73	6.58
IRL	0.00871	0.54	0.53
DR	1.150	0.59	0.58
1 ECU is worth		44.9008	43.99
Depreciation of the ECU in % :		2.06	

When the Belgian franc *appreciates* against the other currencies — as we assumed in the table — the rate of the ECU in terms of the Belgian franc *depreciates* relative to the ECU-related central rate. Thus a *negative* deviation shows up. By contrast, the deviation between the market rate and the central rate of the ECU in terms of a given currency is positive when that currency depreciates against the other ones.

---

[6] See Jean-Jacques Rey: 'Some comments on the merits and limits of the indicator of divergence in the EMS', in *Revue de la Banque*, No 1, 1982.

A reading of the table reveals the following:

(i) The 2.25% depreciation of all the EEC currencies against the Belgian franc translates into a depreciation of the ECU in Belgian francs of approximately 2.06%. This is less than 2.25% because, in the value of the ECU expressed in Belgian francs, the Belgian franc component (3.85) is necessarily a fixed value: the Belgian franc cannot depreciate against itself.

(ii) The ratio of the BFR 3.85 component to the market rate of the ECU in terms of Belgian francs represents the weight of the Belgian franc in the ECU basket. The greater a currency's weight in the ECU is, the less the value of the ECU in terms of that currency will be influenced by variations in the exchange rates of the other currencies making up the ECU;

(iii) The weight of a currency of the ECU is a variable since the market rate of the ECU can change. It tends to increase when the currency in question appreciates; it decreases when the currency depreciates.

Table III-3 gives the maximum divergence spreads and the divergence thresholds for all the EMS currencies.

TABLE III-3

Maximum divergence spreads and divergence thresholds since 17 September 1984

(1) Currency	(2) Maximum spread (as %)	(3) Divergence threshold 75% of (2)
BFR/LFR	±2.06	±1.545
DM	±1.53	±1.148
HFL	±2.02	±1.515
DKR	±2.19	±1.643
FF	±1.82	±1.365
LIT	±5.40	±4.050
IRL	±2.22	±1.665

In short, the divergence indicator (DI) measures the degree of movement of a specific currency against its maximum divergence spread. It is obtained, for a specific currency:

(i) first by calculating the premium (P) or discount (D) shown by the market rate of the ECU in terms of that currency against its ECU-related central rate;

(ii) and then by comparing the result obtained with the maximum divergence spread (MDS).

In order to permit a comparison of movements in the divergence indicators for each of the currencies participating in the EMS, the maximum divergence spread for each currency is assigned an index of 100. The indicator will therefore be expressed by a figure ranging between 0 and 100. A currency reaches its divergence threshold when the indicator displays the figure of 75.

Expressed as a formula, the indicator is calculated as follows:

$$P \text{ or } D = \frac{\text{ECU market} - \text{ECU central}}{\text{ECU central}} \times 100$$

$$DI = \frac{P \text{ or } D}{MDS} \times 100$$

The following example illustrates this calculation.

Data

Rate of the ECU in terms of the BFR on 17 June 1982: 45.2961

ECU-related central rate of the BFR at that time: 44.9704

Maximum divergence spread of the BFR: 2.0668%

Calculation

$$P = \frac{45.2961 - 44.9704}{44.9704} \times 100 = 0.72\%$$

$$DI = \frac{0.72}{2.0668} \times 100 = 35$$

As a general rule, a currency will reach its divergence threshold before reaching its bilateral limit against another currency. This is not however a mathematical necessity. The way the indicator is constructed allows it to stay at certain moments on this side of its threshold after the bilateral limit against another currency has been reached. To some [7] this possibility represents an anomaly and a defect in the construction of the indicator, but the reproach is not very well grounded.

For when a currency reaches its intervention limits against another one, this automatically sets in motion the obligation to intervene. No other signal is needed. But another type of signal — such as the crossing of its threshold by the divergence indicator — may nevertheless be useful to indicate that a particular currency deviates in a systematic fashion from all the others, that the authorities concerned should pay attention to this systematic divergence, and that they are presumed to take correcting measures against it.

The *'presumption to act'* which the crossing of the divergence threshold entails is the result of a compromise between those who felt that this signal ought to trigger compulsory actions — e.g. interventions — by the central bank concerned and those for whom this should only set in motion a consultation procedure.

The measures that the authorities of the country concerned are presumed to take can assume different forms, namely:

(i) *Diversified intervention:* this means intervention on the foreign exchange market in diverse currencies rather than in the single currency which would deviate most from

---

[7] See the article by L. Spaventa in *The International Monetary System under flexible exchange rates*, edited by R. Cooper *et al.*, op. cit.

the currency of the country concerned; diversified intervention should allow a better sharing of the burden of intervention among the various Community currencies.

(ii) *Measures of domestic monetary policy:* these include, among others, action bearing on interest rates, which can have a direct influence on capital flows and contribute to relaxing tensions, as experience with the snake repeatedly showed.

(iii) *Change of the central rate:* while the operation of the EMS itself ought to contribute to reducing divergences among participating economies, it cannot prevent real disparities from subsisting and possibly requiring exchange rate adjustments.

(iv) *Other economic policy measures:* these could include, for instance, measures of fiscal policy or of incomes policy.

In case such measures are not taken by the country concerned because of special circumstances, the reasons for this 'failure to act' must be given to the other authorities, particularly in the framework of the 'consultation between central banks', which has been in existence since 1964 and which the Bremen European Council of July 1978 decided to intensify. If need be, consultations then take place in the appropriate Community bodies, including the Council of Ministers.

The divergence indicator mechanism has thus added two important new features to the snake mechanisms: there is for the first time an *objective basis for triggering* consultation between competent authorities; obviously this goes a step farther than to affirm the principle of consultation which in other respects would be left to the participants' initiative. Besides, this mechanism allows the singling out of the currency which deviates most from the average of the others, and thus locates responsibilities more clearly, which makes for a fairer allocation of the burden of adjustment.

3. The ECU and its functions

(a) The ECU is at the centre of the EMS. It is a composite monetary unit, made up of a basket of specified amounts of each currency.

As Table III-4 indicates, the relative weights of the various currencies in the ECU have changed since the EMS came into operation. This is not surprising since these weights depend not only upon the number of units of each currency in the ECU (first column), which is fixed, but also on the respective values of these currencies, which vary with a realignment of parities. As one can see, the weights in the ECU of currencies which were revalued in the EMS (namely the mark, the guilder, and also the pound sterling, whose notional central rate in the ECU was revalued several times in consequence of the strong appreciation of sterling on the exchange market after 13 March 1979) have increased to the detriment of the other currencies, as long as the composition of the ECU-basket was not revised.

Such changes in the weighting scheme resulting from parity changes could well produce the result that eventually the relative weights would no longer obey the economic criteria by which they had been determined at the outset. For this reason the system had pro-

TABLE III-4

Composition of the ECU

	(A) Between 13.3.1979 and 16.9.1984			(B) Since 17.9.1984 [3]	
	Number of units of national currencies	Weighting on 13.3.1979 [1]	Weighting on 21.3.1983 [2]	Number of units of national currencies	Weighting on 17.9.1984
DM	0.828	33.0	37.38	0.719	32.0
FF	1.150	19.8	16.93	1.310	19.0
UKL	0.0885	13.3	14.05	0.0878	15.0
HFL	0.286	10.5	11.46	0.256	10.1
LIT	109.0	9.5	7.86	140.000	10.2
BFR	3.660	9.2	8.25	3.710	8.2
DKR	0.217	3.1	2.70	0.219	2.7
IRL	0.00759	1.2	1.06	0.00871	1.2
LFR	0.140	0.4	0.32	0.140	0.3
DR	–	–	–	1.150	1.3
		100.0	100.0		100.0

[1] When the EMS came into operation.
[2] Following the latest realignment.
[3] Following the revision of the ECU-basket.

vided from the beginning, by the Resolution of the European Council of 5 December 1978 (see Annex 2, Document 3, 2.3), that the weights of the currencies making up the ECU would be reexamined and, if necessary, revised by a modification of the currency 'bundles' in the basket, every fifth year or on request if the weight of any currency should have changed by 25%.

This examination was held in 1984 and found that a revision was timely. On 15 September 1984 the Council decided, upon a proposal from the Commission and after consulting the Monetary committee and the Board of governors of the FECOM, to revise the composition of the ECU. [8] Furthermore, the Greek government took this opportunity to request the inclusion of the drachma in the ECU, in application of the provisions contained in the Treaty of accession of the Hellenic Republic. The Council welcomed the Greek request, noting that 'for Greece, the inclusion of the drachma in the ECU fits into the framework of a medium term policy aimed at an increased convergence of the economic evolution of this country towards that of the other countries of the Community'.

In accordance with the Resolution of 5 December 1978, this revision did not modify the external value of the ECU, nor did it affect the bilateral parities within the EMS. Even the ECU-related central rates of the currencies participating in the exchange rate mechanism remained unchanged by the revision: this latter result was obtained through a modification of the notional ECU central rate of the pound sterling.

---

[8] See Council Regulation (EEC) No 2626/84 of 15 September 1984. See Document 12 in Annex 2.

(b) In the EMS the ECU is used:

(i) as the denominator (*numéraire*) for the determination of central rates in the exchange rate mechanism;

(ii) as the reference unit for the construction and the operation of the divergence indicator;

(iii) as the denominator for operations performed both in the intervention and the credit mechanism;

(iv) as a means of settlement between the monetary authorities of the EEC.

To serve as a means of settlement, an initial supply of ECU was provided by the FECOM against the deposit of 20% of gold and 20% of dollar reserves held by central banks.

This operation took the form of renewable three-month revolving swaps, thus bypassing legal problems concerning the ownership of national currency reserves. The value of the reserve assets deposited with the FECOM is determined in the following way:

(i) for gold, the average of the prices recorded daily at the two London fixings during the previous six calendar months, without exceeding the average of the two fixings noted the working day before last of the period;

(ii) for the dollar, the market rate two working days prior to the value date.

At the beginning of each quarter, when they renew the swap arrangements, central banks make with the FECOM the necessary adjustments to ensure that each central bank's deposit always represents at least 20% of its gold and dollar reserves. Moreover the quantity of ECU issued is adjusted according to changes in the market price of gold or in the exchange rate of the dollar. Table III-5 illustrates the mechanism of ECU creation during the first five years of the EMS.

Functions (i) and (ii) of the ECU were commented upon in the previous section. Functions (iii) and (iv) require another word of explanation. The *denomination in ECU of the intervention and credit operations* carries with it an exchange risk for both the creditor and the debtor central banks, because the value in national currency of the debts and claims will be influenced by the behaviour of all currencies in the basket. For as soon as the central rate of one currency of the system is adjusted, the rates of the ECU in terms of all the system's currencies are modified. Moreover, the rate of the ECU is also influenced by movements in the rate of the pound sterling, which for the time being does not take part in the exchange rate mechanism. Thus the creditor and debtor central banks incur the risk, in the value in national currency of their ECU-denominated claims and debts, of suffering from actions taken by other monetary authorities, while formerly each country was alone responsible for the rate of conversion of its currency into EMUA. By choosing to denominate in ECU the intervention and credit operations, the system has thus introduced the notion of Community burden-sharing in respect to the exchange rate risk.

Finally the ECU serves as a *means of settlement* between the EMS central banks. The ECU acquired by central banks, through the methods described above, must be used primarily to settle debts arising from intervention in Community currencies, with the proviso that a creditor central bank is not obliged to accept ECU in settlement of its claim over and above 50% of the value of the claim. As to the remuneration of ECU

TABLE III-5

The creation of ECU by swap operations

Swap operations starting in	Gold transfers (million ounces)	US dollar transfers ('000 million)	Gold price (ECU per ounce)	USD 1 = ... ECU	Counterpart in ECU ('000 million)		
					Gold	US dollars	Total
April 1979	80.7	13.4	165	0.75	13.3	10.0	23.3
July 1979 [1]	85.3	15.9	185	0.73	15.8	11.6	27.4
October 1979	85.3	16.0	211	0.70	18.0	11.3	29.3
January 1980	85.5	15.5	259	0.69	22.2	10.7	32.9
April 1980	85.6	14.4	370	0.77	31.7	11.1	42.8
July 1980	85.6	13.7	419	0.70	35.9	9.6	45.5
October 1980	85.6	13.9	425	0.71	36.4	9.9	46.3
January 1981	85.6	14.5	447	0.75	38.3	10.9	49.2
April 1981	85.7	14.2	440	0.84	37.7	12.0	49.7
July 1981	85.7	12.7	406	0.97	34.8	12.3	47.1
October 1981	85.7	11.5	402	0.91	34.5	10.5	45.0
January 1982	85.7	11.7	368	0.92	31.6	10.7	42.3
April 1982	85.7	10.5	327	1	28.1	10.5	38.6
July 1982	85.7	9.9	324	1.05	27.8	10.3	38.1
October 1982	85.7	10.0	367	1.08	31.5	10.8	42.3
January 1983	85.7	10.0	429	1.02	36.7	10.2	47.0
April 1983	85.7	10.5	452	1.07	38.8	11.2	50.0
July 1983	85.7	10.5	465	1.13	39.9	11.8	51.7
October 1983	85.7	10.6	477	1.15	40.9	12.2	53.1
January 1984	85.7	10.6	461	1.24	39.5	13.1	52.6
April 1984	85.7	10.8	452	1.17	38.7	12.7	51.4
July 1984	85.7	10.6	460	1.26	39.5	13.3	52.8

[1] The Bank of England transferred 20% of its gold and dollar reserves from July 1979. The Bank of Greece has made no transfer.
Source: Monthly reports of the agent of the FECOM.

assets, a net user of ECU (that is to say a central bank whose ECU assets are smaller than its forward sales of ECU to the FECOM on account of the revolving swap arrangement) will be required to pay interest to the FECOM, while a central bank which is a net holder of ECU will be paid, by the FECOM, interest on the proportion of its ECU assets exceeding its forward sales. The interest rate is equal to the arithmetic mean of the official discount rates of all the EEC central banks, weighted in accordance with their respective currencies' weights in the ECU.

It should be noted that the rules concerning the creation and the utilization of ECU include for the time being transitional elements that were supposed to be applicable during the initial phase of the system only. In particular, given that the swaps have to be renewed each quarter and are to be unwound after two years unless a decision to the contrary is taken unanimously, the ECU necessarily leads, during this initial phase, a precarious existence, and its legal basis does not correspond to the goal of a 'full utilization of the ECU as a reserve asset and as a means of settlement', which in the constitutive texts was foreseen for the second phase of the EMS.

4. The European Monetary Fund and the existing credit mechanisms

The December 1978 agreement at the European Council of Brussels provided for the future consolidation of all the existing credit mechanisms inside a European Monetary Fund which was to be set up within two years. The creation of this EMF was considered to be part of the institutional phase of the EMS, whose realization has been put off. In the meantime the existing mechanisms, most of which preceded the EMS, continue to function after having undergone substantial adjustments with respect to their volume and, for some, their duration.

(a) Very short-term financing

Very short-term credit facilities, in amounts that are in principle unlimited, are granted to each other by participating central banks, through the FECOM, in order to permit intervention in Community currencies. Operations making use of these facilities are denominated in ECU. The debtor and creditor interest rates are equal to the rates applicable to net users and net holders of ECU assets respectively.

For the purpose of the EMS, the duration of this type of financing has been extended to 45 days from the end of the intervention month, as against 30 days previously. Besides, provision has been made that the financing can be automatically renewed for three months, on condition that the total debt outstanding should never exceed a ceiling equal to the debtor quota of the central bank concerned under the short-term monetary support arrangement (which is dealt with hereafter), and provided this does not result in the relevant debt remaining continuously outstanding for six consecutive months. This ceiling may be raised and the date of repayment postponed with the agreement of the creditor or creditors of the FECOM.

(b) Short-term monetary support

The purpose of this mechanism is to help meet financing needs arising from temporary balance-of-payments deficits which might be caused by unforeseen difficulties or by lack of synchronization between cyclical phases of the economies. It is based on a system of debtor and creditor quotas which determine for each central bank the amounts of its borrowing entitlement and financing obligation. Where circumstances so justify, a central bank may benefit, with the others' agreement, from a 'debtor rallonge' which allows it to increase beyond its debtor quota the amount of the monetary support it can draw upon. As a general rule, a single central bank will not be able to obtain more than one-half of the total amount of debtor rallonges.

At the time of the creation of the EMS, the quotas and rallonges provided by the short-term monetary support arrangement as it existed then (it had been adjusted several times since its birth on 9 February 1970) were raised in accordance with the resolution of the

Brussels European Council. The maximum lending capacity of the mechanism now stands at 14 000 million ECU [9] as against less than 6 000 million previously.

Table III-6 gives these various amounts.

TABLE III-6

Short-term monetary support

	Quotas		Distribution in % of the total
	Debtor	Creditor	
	(in million ECU)		
A. Amounts of the :			
Deutsche Bundesbank	1 740	3 480	22.03
Banque de France	1 740	3 480	22.03
Bank of England	1 740	3 480	22.03
Banca d'Italia	1 160	2 320	14.67
Nederlandsche Bank	580	1 160	7.34
Banque Nationale de Belgique	580	1 160	7.34
Danmarks Nationalbank	260	520	3.29
Central Bank of Ireland	100	200	1.27
Total	7 900	15 800	100.00

B. Amounts of the rallonges:

The total of the creditor rallonges, as well as the total of debtor rallonges, can reach a maximum of 8 800 million ECU.

These credits were previously granted for a duration of three months, renewable once at the request of the beneficiary central bank. With the EMS the possibility of a further three-month extension has been introduced. Normally the short-term monetary support is denominated in the currency of the creditor central bank, but it must be denominated in ECU when it is granted in the form of a prolongation of a debt contracted under the very-short-term financing mechanism.

(c) Medium-term financial assistance

The principle of medium-term financial assistance is based on Article 108 of the Rome Treaty. It is granted, by a Council decision, to any Member State that experiences difficulties or is seriously threatened by difficulties with its balance of payments. The mechanism was set up in 1971 and its lending resources were raised by a Council decision of 21 December 1978 in order to meet the requirements of the EMS.

---

[9] This figure corresponds to the maximum amount of credit that could be obtained in this system with a configuration of borrowers and lenders that would make full use of the system's potential. This amount is necessarily smaller than the sum of the quotas and debtor rallonges since not all central banks can be simultaneously debtors.

Each Member State is required to grant this type of credit only up to a specific commitment ceiling. The total amount of these ceilings, which are listed in Table III-7, was raised to 14 100 million ECU as against 5 450 million previously. The maximum lending capacity of this mechanism stands now at 11 000 million ECU. [10]

TABLE III-7

Commitment ceilings in the medium-term financial assistance

	in million ECU	in % of the total
FR of Germany	3 105	22.02
Belgium	1 000	7.09
Denmark	465	3.30
France	3 105	22.02
Ireland	180	1.28
Italy	2 070	14.68
Luxembourg	35	0.25
The Netherlands	1 035	7.34
United Kingdom	3 105	22.02
Total	14 100	100.00

As a general rule, no Member State can be granted loans amounting to more than 50% of the total amount of the commitment ceilings. Moreover, this financial assistance is conditional, and the country which benefits from it must subscribe to certain economic and monetary engagements. Medium-term financial assistance is denominated in ECU and is granted for a period of between two and five years.

5. Other aspects of the EMS

It is appropriate to mention here two aspects of the EMS which do not belong to the strictly monetary sphere, and respectively pertain to less prosperous Member States and to the 'agri-monetary' implications of the system.

(a) Measures designed to strengthen the economies of the less prosperous Member States of the EMS

The durability of the EMS will depend on the convergence of the Member States' economic performances. In the resolution establishing the EMS, the European Council explicitly stated that measures taken at the Community level could and should play a supporting role in strengthening the less prosperous countries' economic potential and in fostering the convergence of economic results.

---

[10] See footnote No 9.

Provision has thus been made for measures that will assist less prosperous Member States, provided they participate fully and effectively in the exchange rate mechanism. But Member States which do not participate fully and effectively in the exchange rate mechanism do not have to contribute to the financing of the system.

These measures consist of the granting of 3% interest rate subsidies on loans made available to those Member States by Community institutions within the framework of the new financial instrument (the New Community Instrument – NCI) and by the European Investment Bank. The loans granted under these conditions may reach a total amount of 1 000 million ECU per year for a period of five years. The cost of interest rate subsidies may not exceed 200 million ECU per year for five years.

Table III-8 shows that the possibilities offered by this system have been fully exploited during the first five years of the EMS.

TABLE III-8

Subsidized loans and EMS subsidies paid out

	Subsidized loans		Interest subsidies paid out	
	Number	Million ECU	Million ECU	% of loans
1979	34	885.4	200.0	22.6
1980	55	1 030.8	197.0	19.1
1981	58	1 017.5	193.2	19.0
1982	34	1 041.4	209.8	20.1
1983	50	1 062.9	200.0	18.8
Total	231	5 038.0	1 000.0	19.8

Source : 'The borrowing and lending activities of the Community in 1983', *European Economy,* No 21, September 1984.

The funds thus made available to less prosperous Member States are to be used mainly for financing selected infrastructure projects and programmes, on the understanding that any direct or indirect distortion of the competitive position of specific industries that might result will have to be avoided.

(b) The agri-monetary implications of the EMS

As we saw in Chapter II, one of the rules of the common agricultural policy (CAP) is the unity of agricultural prices in the EEC which—at least for agricultural products subject to the intervention regime—have been fixed in European units of account every year since 1964. In the case of adjustment of a currency's parity, the logic of the CAP would imply that the prices of agricultural products, expressed in national currency, should be increased by the percentage of devaluation in the country which devalues its currency, or decreased in the country which revalues its currency.

But member country governments were not prepared to accept these domestic consequences of a monetary adjustment, because they deemed such consequences to be inflationary in the first case and detrimental to farmers' interests in the second. This is the origin of the monetary compensatory amounts (MCAs) that were applied for the first time when the French franc devalued in August 1969, and which aim at neutralizing the impact of parity adjustments on agricultural prices in terms of national currency.

With the advent of floating exchange rates there was a risk of new complications. Nevertheless, the decision was made to maintain the unity of agricultural prices in the Community. But it became necessary in consequence to modify the method for converting agricultural units of account into national currencies, in order to prevent prices in national currency of agricultural products from floating as well. This was the origin of the 'green' currencies, which are national currencies whose exchange rate with the European unit of account is stable but adjustable. The 'green' rate, specific for each currency, is the one at which the European unit of account is converted into green currency for the purpose of determining agricultural prices in national currency. The MCA will then reappear in order to offset the difference that for each Community currency may exist between its green rate and its true exchange rate as it emerges from the market. If for instance a given currency depreciates by 10% against the EMUA, but as a result the decision is made to devalue the corresponding green currency by only 5%, the green rate for this currency now exceeds the market rate by 5%, and negative MCAs have to be introduced in the form of import subsidies and export duties.

The advent of the EMS has both simplified the calculation of MCAs and introduced a new complication. The simplification arises from the fact that, for currencies participating in the EMS exchange rate mechanism, MCAs are now fixed and based on the possible difference between the green rate and the central rate, both being related to the ECU. But given that, by reason of the features of the ECU, the adjustment of bilateral parities for a single currency will change the ECU-related central rates for all the currencies in the basket, the MCAs flowing from the parity change of a currency will be, so to speak, partially transferred onto the other currencies, and therefore the new MCAs thus created will be more symmetrical than the former ones, which may facilitate a subsequent dismantling.

The difficulty springs from the fact that for the purpose of the CAP the reference is not the ECU as such but the ECU-related central rate of the currencies which maintain a 2.25% margin among themselves. For these currencies, the MCAs are calculated in function of the spread between the green rate and the central rate, and remain fixed as long as the central rate or the green rate does not change.

For the other currencies (lira, sterling, drachma) the MCAs are variable and computed every week: they are equal to the spread between the green rate of the currency concerned and the mean of its market rates against the EMS currencies. However, unlike a modification of bilateral parities for a currency participating in the exchange rate mechanism, a market variation of the pound sterling does not result in a change in the ECU-related central rates of the other currencies. Therefore, in the case of MCAs which result for the United Kingdom of a variation in the exchange rate of its currency, their partial transfer onto the other currencies will not take place, and the United Kingdom will assume alone the totality of the MCAs flowing from the fluctuations of the pound. It is only through a modification of sterling's notional central rate that a subsequent redistribution of MCAs assigned to the United Kingdom between two realignments can be operated.

This underlines how difficult it can be to make an integrated agricultural common market coexist with a common market for currencies which is not integrated.

6. Conditions for the proper operation of the EMS [11]

The mechanisms that were just formally described are, one might say, the constitution of the EMS rather than its real content. The latter depends more on the actual manner in which these mechanisms operate in reality and allow Member States to draw nearer, or not, to the goals pursued. The next chapter will discuss the experience of five years of EMS functioning and will thus permit a better appraisal of its real substance.

From the start however, it was possible, on the basis of the previous experience with the snake, to state a number of *conditions* for the proper functioning of the EMS mechanisms. And the *objections* that were raised at the time against the EMS essentially gave vent to doubts about the possibility of these conditions coinciding.

(a) A convergence of economic situations

First of all, the EMS will only last, and work, if it is sustained by the achievement of a greater degree of convergence among Member States' economic performances, in respect mainly to prices and costs, and by the policies, monetary, fiscal and bearing on the rate of change of incomes, that are necessary for such convergence. *Important divergences existed at the outset:* the inflation rate for instance, for the year 1978, ranged from 2.7% in Germany to 12.2% in Italy. (This spread of almost ten points, as we shall see below, was further increased under the influence of the second oil shock.) The *principal objections* that were raised against the EMS at the time were based on the existence of those divergences. The disparity of economic situations, it was felt, was too great to permit the erection of a system of stable exchange rates. Such excessive divergences, according to several of the EMS' critics, would have *three possible consequences:*

(i)   either the system would rapidly explode, because its rigidity would not permit it to accommodate situations that would diverge too much; or

(ii) it would hold together after a fashion, but this would have deflationary consequences for the participating economies, and thus exert a negative impact on employment, either by forcing high-inflation countries to adopt restrictive policies, or because the parity of weak currencies would be 'pulled upward' by the German mark and the countries concerned would suffer more and more in their competitiveness; or

(iii) it would have an inflationary impact, for it would force strong-currency countries with a low rate of inflation to import inflation from their weaker partners, both via the prices of their imports from those partners and because the support of weaker currencies would lead them, through purchasing these currencies against their own, to increase unduly their own monetary base.

---

[11] On this subject see J. van Ypersele: 'Operating principles and procedures of the EMS', in *The European Monetary System: Its Promises and Prospects*, The Brookings Institution, Washington DC, 1979.

(*a.1.*) The first objection was, of course, disproved by the facts. The EMS did not explode and it is therefore possible to speak about it today otherwise than in the past tense. The fact that it could hold together in spite of the divergence of economic situations was due partly to an unusual set of circumstances, as we shall see in the next chapter, and partly to its being far less rigid than its detractors claimed, and being managed with the flexibility allowed by its mechanisms. This *flexible management* of the EMS is in fact a second condition of its good operation—we shall come back to it shortly—and it provided a possible answer to this first objection at the time it was raised.

(*a.2.*) The second objection—the necessarily deflationary impact of the EMS—partly rested upon a view that was still shared by some at the time but is more and more rejected nowadays. Contrary to what the well-known 'Phillips curve' seemed to imply, there is no stable trade-off between inflation and unemployment, nor is it necessary to accept a supplement of inflation in order to get faster economic growth. On the contrary, countries which succeeded in maintaining a relatively low inflation rate were often gratified, in the medium term, with better results for growth and employment.

This, however, does not preclude transitional problems for some less prosperous Member States with a high inflation rate like Ireland and Italy, which may find it difficult to switch to more restrictive policies of demand management. It is precisely to meet this type of difficulty that the EMS has made provisions for measures that would transfer resources toward less prosperous Member States, as we have seen.

A less primitive version of the 'deflationary' objection consisted of claiming that, in the EMS, weak-currency countries with a high inflation rate would see their parity 'pulled upward' against third currencies by the system's strong currencies, more especially by the German mark, and that therefore their competitiveness would be adversely affected. This version of the deflationary objection cannot be refuted in the abstract. But it is only valid inasmuch as the strong-currency country refuses to take internal measures to prevent an excessive increase in the value of its currency and also refuses, under this assumption, to have its currency revalued in relation to other currencies whose inflationary performance is less favourable.

The answer to this is that the system of the ECU divergence indicator was precisely designed to induce countries whose currency is diverging to take the domestic measures that will cause this divergence to subside. Furthermore, experience with the snake had already shown that needed changes of the central rates could be carried out efficiently and flexibly.

(*a.3.*) As to the objection according to which the EMS would have an inflationary bias for the strong-currency countries and for Germany in particular, it cannot be refuted in the abstract either. Everything depends upon how the system will operate in practice. This danger may exist to the extent that, as at the end of the Bretton Woods system, timely changes of parities would be resisted. But to the extent that, as in the experience with the mini-snake, parity changes are carried out in time, there should follow no durable swelling of the monetary stock in Germany. Seen from this angle also, flexibility in the operation of the system appears to be an important condition of its adequacy.

These three objections raised against the EMS at the time of its birth were all grounded in a double fear or, for some, a double conviction:

(i) First, the fear that the exchange rate mechanism aimed at achieving external stability in the EMS would not be complemented or sustained by a sufficient convergence of effort toward internal stability. This fear is well-founded, for one must acknowledge that by itself the exchange rate mechanism can only play a limited role if it happens to be the only available instrument for coordination. Thus one has to admit that the medium-term survival of the EMS as well as its good functioning require the stabilization of exchange rates to be paired with a more effective coordination of economic policies and a better convergence of results.

(ii) Secondly, the fear (or the conviction) that the management of the system would be too rigid and would not allow the needed parity changes to be carried out in time.

The coordination needed for the good functioning of the EMS should take place particularly in the following domains:

(i) The coordination of monetary policies should aim to ensure the compatibility of Member States' domestic monetary objectives with the exchange rate objectives, and with the broader economic objectives they might be assigned by the Council of the European Communities. In this regard, it appears preferable to focus on the domestic components of monetary creation rather than on one or the other measure of the monetary stock.

(ii) The coordination of policies for the management of aggregate demand can also play an important role in the convergence of results. One should recall in this respect the efforts of concerted economic action undertaken at Bremen in July 1978, which aimed at modulating the various countries' expansionary stances according to their inflation and balance-of-payments situations. In this context it was the country with the strongest economy at the time which took the most expansionary measures. This helped weaker economies make the necessary adjustments, and was a factor which partly accounted for the good operation of the EMS in the following years.

(iii) Other elements of domestic economic policy also have an important role to play in this search for convergence. These last few years, the European authorities have paid increasing attention to the changes in private incomes and wage costs, as well as to policies (with regard *inter alia* to wage indexation) which might bend those evolutions in order to make them converge more.

(iv) Finally, the operation of the divergence indicator should also play a role in the coordination of policies. It does not represent merely a compromise on the question of whether compulsory intervention should be triggered by the rate of the ECU or of the bilateral parities. It was also explicitly designed as an objective indicator for triggering the coordination of policies. Such a signal did not exist in the snake. It is therefore important to learn to use it well and to use it effectively as an element in a balanced process of adjustment, which early in the game warns where divergences are appearing and induces the country concerned to take corrective action.

(b) A flexible operation of the system

The flexibility of the EMS is an important condition for its proper functioning, the more so at the beginning of the system, when the coordination of policies and the convergence of results were still very much lacking and when therefore the exchange rate mechanism alone had to absorb the tensions that could arise from the initial divergence. This necessary flexibility can be attained in the EMS in different ways:

(i) The exchange rates are 'stable but adjustable', and the adjustments must reflect real and persisting disparities. Thus it greatly matters to avoid the excessive rigidity of Bretton Woods and to 'dedramatize' parity changes.

The experience with the snake during its last three years was a rather positive one in this respect. Several adjustments took place when the exchange markets were calm. Some involved a general realignment. This, for instance, was the case with the October 1976 realignment, which was carefully planned and infused new life into the snake when many outside observers were forecasting its imminent demise.

The realignment which occurred two years later was also successful. It was a kind of pre-emptive strike which anticipated likely market tensions as the deadline of 1 January 1979, the date set initially for launching the EMS, drew near. This operation permitted the system to start in a quiet way, first unofficially in January 1979, then officially on 13 March.

(ii) Possible movements within the authorized fluctuation margins are another element of flexibility, in particular for the currencies which did not belong to the snake in 1978 and which were given the option of a 6% margin. This second element of flexibility also allows a more efficient use of the first element, namely the adjustment of central rates, in a manner which may deter speculation.

One often hears the opinion that a system of stable exchange rates encourages speculation, which cannot but gain from it. This is inaccurate. To the extent that parity adjustments are limited and do not exceed the width of the authorized margin of fluctuation, speculation against a currency will not necessarily gain from a parity adjustment. If indeed the currency was at its floor rate before the adjustment and is traded at its ceiling after the adjustment, and if the adjustment is inferior to the margin (that is 2.25%, and 6% for the lira), speculators will lose.

Experience with the snake has shown that central rates may be adjusted by as much as 4% without having much effect on the market rates, to the extent that, following the adjustment, the devalued currency switches positions with the strong currency inside the authorized fluctuation margin.

(c) A more stable relationship between the dollar and European currencies

To obtain a greater stability in the rate of the dollar *vis-à-vis* the ECU is not an absolute condition for the success of the EMS, for the EMS was created, in part, to remedy the

69

disadvantages which the instability of the dollar brought to Europe, by allowing the impact of the dollar weakness to spread over a broader monetary zone. But it remains true that movements of the dollar often aggravate tensions within the EMS and that, *a contrario*, the smooth launching of the EMS was made easier by the relative stability of the dollar at the beginning of 1979.

It is proper to meet *two more objections* raised against the creation of the EMS. One consisted of saying that, in the monetary field, progress is possible only on a world scale, under the IMF aegis, and should necessarily include agreements over the dollar.

One can answer first that obviously a return of the dollar to more stability will be an important contribution to monetary equilibrium, both for Europe and for the world. We emphasized earlier how excessive fluctuations of the dollar added to divergences between European currencies. One should therefore pursue and encourage all the efforts undertaken with the United States to achieve a greater stability of the dollar in relation to European currencies. But we deem such efforts to be complementary to, and not a substitute for, intra-European efforts.

Furthermore, we are convinced that it is feasible to return to stable and adjustable exchange rates among European currencies, particularly if these efforts are accompanied by a better coordination of economic policies. But to aim at such stability world-wide would not be realistic. Capital flows have become too important to allow a return to the stability of Bretton Woods. A more realistic alternative consists of setting up large zones of stability, within which stable exchange rates can be maintained and between which fluctuations could possibly be controlled more effectively. One should mention in addition that the adoption of stricter rules on a regional basis does not prevent the countries concerned from observing the more general rules defined for IMF countries.

A last objection raised against the EMS was that it took too much freedom of manoeuvre away from participating countries and implied a transfer of sovereign rights.

But recent events affecting European currencies, tossed about by the waves of the dollar, vividly showed the effective limits of national sovereignty in monetary matters. It seems on the contrary that, through the organization of a European monetary area, European countries could recapture together part of the sovereignty they have lost individually.

Besides, when the IMF imposes, in a difficult situation, very constraining conditions, are some countries not compelled to accept at certain times transfers of relative sovereignty that are in fact far more important? And is it therefore too ambitious to request much more modest transfers at the European level, especially when those transfers are on a par with measures that strengthen European solidarity?

Chapter IV —
Five years with the EMS

1. The changing international environment

(a) The machinery described in the preceding chapter has been in operation for more than five years, and the present chapter will appraise this experience in order to draw some possible lessons for the future of the EMS.

In conducting this appraisal one must keep in mind above all the two objectives assigned to the EMS by its creators, namely a greater stability of exchange rates between European currencies on the one hand, and a better convergence of participating economies towards internal stability on the other hand. The pursuit of this twofold objective by the EMS can be seen as a further application of the principle, stated in the 1970 Werner report, of a parallel progress toward monetary integration and toward convergence of economic policies.

The main question to be asked is to what extent the EMS mechanisms succeeded or not in bringing European economies and currencies closer. However, for a correct appraisal of the extent of this *rapprochement*, one would ideally want to compare it with the evolution that might have taken place had the EMS not existed. Such hypothetical reconstruction is unfortunately not feasible, but one cannot fail to observe nevertheless that, during the period under consideration, the international environment was greatly disturbed and that factors likely to increase divergences among European economies were often operating.

(b) Neither is it superfluous to recall that, when the decisions to create the EMS were taken in 1978, the economic outlook for the European Community was much brighter than it became afterwards. Indeed, by the end of 1978, the European Community as a whole had eliminated the current account deficit caused by the first oil shock, and was in fact running a surplus of some USD 17 000 million, while the global surplus of OPEC countries had virtually vanished. Moreover, the terms of trade for industrialized countries as a whole and for the European Community in particular had considerably improved since 1974. Inflation rates, although still too high in some Member States, had nevertheless fallen everywhere in the Community, and their divergence had narrowed. Finally, the strong disparities in balance-of-payments behaviour which had been a feature of European economies at the beginning of the decade were also reduced.

71

In short, when the EMS first saw the light, not only was the external position of the Community as a whole reasonably strong, but the conditions for a greater exchange rate stability among Member States were more auspicious than they had been for years. The smooth functioning of the EMS during its first few months was certainly made easier by these favourable circumstances.

The coming of the second petroleum shock shattered this peaceful climate. Once again the terms of trade moved against the European Community; most of its members were plunged anew in current account deficits; and inflationary pressures were intensified. But the balance-of-payments impact of this new wave of oil price increases was unevenly distributed, since some member countries were more dependent on imported oil than others; and because of national differences regarding the capacity or the resolve to resist new inflationary pressures, inflation rates started diverging once again. Thus, a clear effect of the second petroleum shock in Europe was to invigorate the factors of economic divergence among Member States and to inflict new tensions on their exchange relationships.

(c) Let us finally underline the changes in the behaviour of the dollar and in the policy followed by US authorities with respect to the dollar since the beginning of the EMS.

During the first six months of the system, the foreign exchange markets—at least the dollar-mark market—were in a state of relative calm, following the measures in support of the dollar jointly taken by the United States, Germany and Switzerland in the autumn of 1978. This showed up in the daily variability of the dollar-mark spot exchange rate, measured for instance, over a year, by the proportion of working days during which the rate varied by more than 0.5%. Thus measured, the daily variability was clearly smaller in 1979 than in 1978, but it went up again over the next two years, reaching 54% in 1981. During 1981, the increase in the daily variability of the dollar-mark spot rate was accompanied by a like evolution in the exchange rates of the dollar with sterling and with the yen respectively. [1]

Starting in October 1979, the US authorities adopted new techniques of monetary control, whose virtues were disputed, but which undoubtedly gave rise to a much greater volatility of American interest rates and of the differential between US and European rates. This evolution, along with the short-term capital movements it provoked, produced wider fluctuations in 1980 of the exchange rate of the dollar *vis-à-vis* European currencies (− 10% from May 1979 to January 1980, + 13% from January to April 1980 and − 10% from April to July 1980).

Finally, from July 1980 on, the dollar was carried along a steeply rising trend relative to European currencies, virtually without interruption until August 1981, and between these two dates it gained 45% against the ECU. Then it went down by approximately 10% until November 1981, and resumed its upward trend thereafter.

The United States' monetary policy was relaxed in the second half of 1982, which induced for the dollar a brief spell of weakness on the foreign exchange market. But

[1] See *Fifty-second annual report*, Bank for International Settlements, Basle, 14.6.1982.

starting in 1983 the increase in the Federal Government's budget deficit led to a renewed tightening of monetary conditions, and the dollar quickly resumed its upward climb.

Let us also note that the yen too has fluctuated widely in relation to the ECU: it lost almost 30% of its value between August 1978 and November 1979, then regained the lost ground between February 1980 and August 1981. Afterwards it was on a slightly downward trend until September 1982, due to substantial outflows of Japanese private funds attracted to the United States by better-paying investment opportunities. The yen recovered thereafter—at a time interest rates were falling in the United States—and since the beginning of 1983 it has followed the dollar on its upward trend.

The movement since 1979 of these two great currencies and of the SDR in relation to the ECU appears in Graph A, which shows that, in relation to the ECU, the yen and the

GRAPH A

Exchange rates of the USD, the yen and the SDR against the ECU

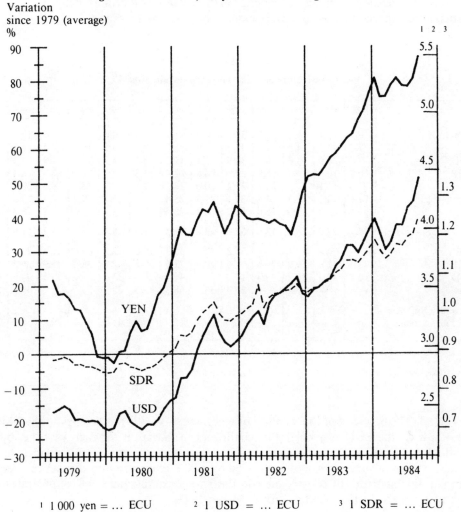

¹ 1 000 yen = ... ECU   ² 1 USD = ... ECU   ³ 1 SDR = ... ECU

73

dollar had reached, in September 1984, about twice the lowest levels touched in, respectively, February and July 1980.

Undoubtedly such large fluctuations in exchange rates have combined with the divergence due to the second oil shock to cause growing strains inside a zone of relative monetary stability like the EMS, at any rate during its first three years. Since 1982 on the other hand, the strength of the dollar and the corresponding relative weakness of the mark have on the average been a contributing factor in relaxing potential tensions inside the EMS.

2. The EMS and external stability

(a) Nevertheless, the EMS effectively held fast against those shocks and succeeded in absorbing the tensions. The objective of a relative stabilization of exchange rates among participating currencies was to a large extent achieved, as shown in Table IV-1.

TABLE IV-1

Yearly variability of major currencies against the ECU [1]

	1972	1973	1974	1975	1976	1977	1978	1979	1980	1981	1982	1983	1984
BFR/LFR	9.7	11.1	16.0	9.9	35.1	6.3	11.7	8.1	8.6	7.9	22.6	10.0	6.2
DM	7.6	42.8	14.8	7.8	37.2	11.9	11.8	8.2	9.2	18.8	16.4	6.4	3.1
HFL	9.0	26.9	13.8	6.4	36.9	5.5	11.2	8.7	4.2	20.1	17.9	4.5	3.2
DKR	16.7	10.9	14.4	5.9	29.9	30.8	7.4	31.3	4.3	8.0	7.9	8.3	4.7
FF	11.5	11.1	21.3	24.1	30.4	10.0	18.6	7.1	5.9	13.2	29.4	20.3	2.4
LIT	11.6	43.1	27.3	14.4	39.1	21.2	25.4	9.4	17.1	20.9	8.5	13.5	4.6
IRL	33.5	42.8	19.9	26.6	61.9	10.8	22.4	7.4	8.8	6.1	4.2	18.3	3.9
EMS average	14.2	27.0	18.2	13.6	38.6	13.8	15.5	11.4	8.3	13.6	15.3	11.6	4.0
SFR	—	—	—	—	36.8	47.3	51.3	10.0	12.5	65.6	19.9	22.1	14.3
UKL	33.5	42.8	19.9	26.6	61.6	10.8	22.4	30.8	42.8	38.6	25.9	36.2	13.7
USD	10.8	47.4	26.3	49.3	17.3	25.7	49.1	26.9	33.0	59.7	43.5	44.7	47.0
Yen	—	—	—	—	29.9	33.9	68.8	83.8	78.7	24.8	27.7	49.2	26.6
Average for these four currencies	—	—	—	—	36.4	29.4	47.9	37.9	41.7	47.2	29.2	38.0	25.4

[1] Standard deviation of end-of-month rates for each currency in ECU, divided by the annual average of such rates. Results multiplied by 1 000.
Source: Commission departments.

In Table IV-1, the index of the stability of a currency—whether it belongs to the EMS or not—*vis-à-vis* the ECU is given by its coefficient of variation for each year, i.e. by the standard deviation of the end-of-month rates of this currency in ECU, divided by the annual average of such rates, and multiplied by 1 000. Exchange rate changes recorded to compute this statistic, of course, include the seven readjustments of central rates that took place in the EMS since its start in March 1979.

This table suggests that:

(i) During the EMS's first two years, the average stability of participating currencies was greater (that is, the index for the EMS average has a smaller value) than in any previous year since 1972.

(ii) A similar claim cannot be made in the absolute for all the participating currencies taken one by one. For most of them it is indeed possible to find one or two years, during the pre-EMS period, for which the index has a smaller value than in 1979 or 1980 (for instance the year 1977 for the Belgian franc). Nevertheless, the overall impression of a greater stability brought by the EMS remains true for each of these currencies with the exception of the Danish krone. The high value of the index for the krone in 1979 is an obvious consequence of the two devaluations which it underwent against the ECU during that year.

(iii) The average instability rises in 1981 and further in 1982, and the value of the index, for the EMS average, nearly overtakes in 1982 its level of 1978. The increase in the value of the index relative to the first two years of the EMS, particularly for the mark, the guilder, the French franc and the lira in 1981, and for the Belgian franc, the mark, the guilder and the French franc in 1982, is a consequence of the realignments in these currencies' central rates which occurred during that period.

(iv) For the EMS average, the instability index regains in 1983 its level of 1979 and it falls further down in 1984: during the latter year, for all the participating currencies taken one by one, the index has a smaller value than in any year over the period 1972-78.

(v) Lastly, the instability of the external environment is shown by the fact that the other large currencies (namely the Swiss franc, the pound sterling, the US dollar and the yen) were subject to average fluctuations against the ECU much wider than the EMS currencies. This comparison clearly brings out the features of the 'islet of monetary stability' which the EMS has been so far.

To back up this claim let us quote another index recently put forward by the European Commission: 'Between 1979 and 1983, the average changes from one month to the next in the exchange rates of the other EMS currencies against the mark (taken as the standard reference currency) ranged from 0.5% to 0.8%; those of the three major non-participating currencies, the dollar, the yen and sterling, were three times as wide: between 2.4% and 2.7%. The average rate of change against the mark of the French franc and the lira, which floated freely before joining the EMS, was reduced by more than half after 1979, in relation to 1974-78; for the French franc, it fell from 1.7% to 0.8%; for the lira, from 2.2% to 0.8%.' [2]

Another statistic suggests that the EMS put an end to the previously observed phenomenon of overshooting.

Indeed, it appears that in countries like Italy and Ireland, which experienced higher inflation than their partners, the decrease in the effective exchange rate, during the period of operation of the EMS, was clearly smaller in yearly average than during the previous

---

[2] See 'Five years of monetary cooperation in Europe', Communication from the Commission to the Council, 2 March 1984.

TABLE IV - 2

Variations in effective exchange rates [1] relative to EMS partners (annual percentages)

	$\dfrac{1979}{1973}$	$\dfrac{1984}{1979}$ (2)	$\dfrac{1980}{1979}$	$\dfrac{1981}{1980}$	$\dfrac{1982}{1981}$	$\dfrac{1983}{1982}$	$\dfrac{1984}{1983}$ (2)
Belgium	+ 1.7	− 2.2	+ 0.2	− 0.2	− 8.3	− 2.2	− 0.2
Denmark	− 0.8	− 2.4	− 6.9	+ 0.2	− 4.1	− 0.8	− 0.4
FR of Germany	+ 6.1	+ 4.7	+ 1.6	+ 3.5	+ 9.1	+ 6.9	+ 2.6
France	− 1.5	− 2.9	+ 1.4	− 0.8	− 6.9	− 6.4	− 1.4
Ireland	− 5.5	− 1.1	+ 0.7	− 0.4	+ 0.1	− 3.9	− 1.9
Italy	− 9.6	− 3.8	− 3.4	− 4.9	− 5.4	− 2.6	− 2.4
The Netherlands	+ 3.1	+ 2.7	+ 1.2	+ 1.3	+ 7.3	+ 3.1	+ 0.8
United Kingdom [3]	− 4.7	+ 2.6	+10.0	+10.2	− 1.5	− 5.5	− 0.4

[1] Export weighting, variable from year to year until 1980.
[2] Forecasts: economic budgets.
[3] In relation to Community countries, October 1984.
Sources: Eurostat and Commission departments.

period, reflecting their less tolerant approach to inflation than before and a greater anxiety to escape, with the EMS's support, from the vicious circles of depreciation-inflation. [3]

(*b*) Evidently this relative stability obtained between the EMS currencies was not fortuitous. It was consciously pursued by the participating countries in their monetary policy, partly through setting interest rates, partly via the exchange rate mechanism and the intervention of central banks aimed at keeping their respective currencies within the limits provided by the mechanism (i.e. 2.25% on either side of the central rate, and 6% in the particular case of the lira).

First let us deal with interest rates. Table IV-3 reveals an interesting phenomenon.

TABLE IV - 3

Short-term interest rates for countries participating in the EMS exchange rate mechanism

	1977	1978	1979	1980	1981	1982	1983	1984
Belgium	7.3	7.3	10.9	14.2	15.6	14.1	10.5	11.9
Denmark	14.5	15.4	12.5	16.9	14.9	16.4	12.0	11.6
FR of Germany	4.3	3.7	6.9	9.5	12.3	8.8	5.8	6.0
France	9.1	7.8	9.7	12.0	15.3	14.6	12.4	12.0
Ireland	8.4	9.9	16.0	16.2	16.6	17.5	14.0	12.8
Italy	14.0	11.5	12.0	17.2	19.7	19.9	18.3	17.3
The Netherlands	4.8	7.0	9.6	10.6	11.8	8.2	5.7	6.1
Mean	8.9	8.9	11.1	13.8	15.2	14.2	11.2	11.1
Standard deviation	4.0	3.7	2.8	3.1	2.7	4.4	4.5	4.0
Coefficient of variation	0.45	0.42	0.26	0.23	0.17	0.31	0.40	0.36

Between 1978 and 1981-82, nominal short-term interest rates followed a strongly upward trend, which can be explained both by the resurgence of inflation in the wake of the

---

[3] See 'Documents relating to the EMS', op. cit. p. 24.

second oil shock and by the restrictive stance taken by American monetary policy, particularly in 1981 and 1982.

Worthier of notice is the fact that the start of the EMS in 1979 seems to have been accompanied, at any rate until 1981, by a certain convergence of nominal interest rates among the countries participating in the exchange rate mechanism. This appears in the movement of the standard deviation, and still more clearly in the trend of the coefficient of variation (i.e. the ratio of the standard deviation to the mean).

This *rapprochement* of short-term interest rates is probably a consequence of the EMS. Differentials across countries can be explained fundamentally by different inflation rates and by differences in balance-of-payments situations and in the state of public finances. However, when the markets do not anticipate a shift of central rates in the near future, short-term capital movements across member countries are mostly guided by nominal interest rate differentials, and the latter become, along with central bank intervention, an important tool of exchange rate policy. [4]

Therefore, owing to the creation of the EMS and to the political will to stabilize exchange rates which it expressed, inflation differentials and the expectations of exchange rate variations which they normally foster tend to lose importance as a determining factor of short-term interest rate differentials. This may explain how such convergence of nominal interest rates happened during the first three years of the EMS while, as we show later, the divergence of inflation rates was in fact increasing. By the same token, if nominal interest rates show a tendency to diverge again in 1982 and 1983, this is probably and in part because the higher frequency of realignments since the last quarter of 1981 led the market to place less faith on the stability of central rates than it did during the EMS's first three years, and therefore to pay less exclusive attention to nominal interest rates.

Let us now deal with the subject of intervention. How important has it been?

We should first make a distinction between intervention in dollars, aimed in principle at dampening fluctuations in the exchange rate of that currency against European currencies, and interventions in EMS currencies, aimed at influencing these currencies' position within the band and at observing fluctuation limits in the system.

This distinction however cannot remain absolute, not only because intervention of the second type sometimes uses dollars, as we shall see below, but also because intervention of the first type can be directed against tensions which, although originating outside the EMS, affect the exchange rates inside the system.

Such tensions can result from the fact that an inflow of short-term capital toward European currencies, or conversely an outflow toward dollar investments, does not affect the European currencies equally. In general, the impact will be stronger on the German mark, if only because this currency is actively traded on the New York market.

Let us assume for instance that the dollar weakens, and that short-term capital takes shelter in the German mark, causing tension between this and other European currencies.

---

[4] See 'Annual Economic Review 1981-82', in *European Economy*, No 10, November 1981, p. 90.

German authorities could then choose to relax those intra-EMS tensions by purchasing other European currencies against their own currency: in this case, the whole system would be 'pulled upward' by the mark and away from the dollar. But the Federal Republic's authorities might also choose to ward off this tension inside the EMS by dealing with its external cause, and by buying dollars against marks.

More recently, prior to the 12 June 1982 realignment, it was the mark which was 'pulled downward' relative to the dollar, due to the fact that several other European currencies were weakening against the dollar.

Whatever the reasons or the forms it took, it appears that intervention by EMS central banks, although substantial, did not exhaust the system's possibilities by a long chalk.

The following table shows how intervention made by the EMS central banks taken together developed semester by semester: [5]

TABLE IV-4

Intervention by the EMS central banks

Semester	Net dollar intervention (USD '000 million)	Gross intervention in Commmunity currencies ('000 million ECU)	
		Total	Of which: notified to FECOM
1979 I	1.6	n.a.	1.0
II	1.0	n.a.	2.0
1980 I	12.0	n.a.	2.2
II	2.0	n.a.	2.3
1981 I	15.8	n.a.	7.6
II	10.0	n.a.	2.3
1982 I	14.9	7.0	1.9
II	11.0	6.0	0.5
1983 I	3.0	22.0	5.3
II	7.0	7.0	1.1
1984 I	4.5	10.0	2.1

Source: FECOM.

Net sales of dollars by the EMS central banks were especially important in 1981 (USD 25 800 million) and 1982 (USD 25 900 million). Over the period going from the beginning of the EMS to 30 June 1984, they reached a total of approximately USD 83 000 million. A large proportion of these operations seems to have been carried out by the

---

[5] Up to a point, the comparison between dollar intervention and intervention in Community currencies which this table shows can be misleading. Indeed, the amounts of dollar intervention listed represent net interventions. Gross sales of dollars were more important: for the period April 79 through June 81 they might have reached USD 50 000 million, as against 32 400 million for net sales. The amounts listed for intervention in Community currencies represent gross intervention: thus they include, among others, the operations by which central banks repurchase their creditors' currencies in order to settle debts arising from intervention carried out previously.

Bundesbank, at least during the first two years of the EMS: between April 1979 and June 1981, its net intervention totalled USD 18 700 million (a sum equivalent to 2.3% of German GDP in 1980), out of a global amount of USD 32 400 for all the EMS central banks taken together. [6]

Until March 1981 the impact of dollar intervention by the EMS central banks was reinforced by intervention in European currencies performed by the Federal Reserve Bank of New York, but in May 1981 the US authorities officially confirmed that, apart from exceptional circumstances, they no longer intended to intervene on the foreign exchange market. However, the Versailles Summit in July 1982 gave an inkling of a possible softening of the American attitude in this matter.

Intervention in Community currencies must be notified to the FECOM to the extent that it is carried out at fluctuation limits, thus being triggered by the EMS basic rules. So-called intra-marginal intervention, on the other hand, is not in principle notified to the FECOM, except where it is financed by transfers of ECU or use of the very short-term financing mechanism, a rather infrequent occurrence.

Intervention in Community currencies notified to the FECOM (thus representing for the most part intervention made at fluctuation limits) was particularly important during the first half of 1981, in support of the mark (in February), of the Belgian franc (in March-April) and of the French franc (in May 1981), as well as during the first half of 1983, where it was needed in February and March in order to prop up the Belgian and French francs, the lira and the Irish pound, prior to the currency realignment of 21 March 1983.

But the total amount of gross intervention in Community currencies much exceeds the amounts notified to the FECOM inasmuch as intramarginal intervention was important, as the data, available from 1982 on, show in the preceding table. Besides, it appears that during the first two years of the EMS' existence, about two thirds of the intervention in Community currencies was intra-marginal, i.e. carried out before intervention limits were reached. [7]

This intervention corresponded to the authorities' desire either to steer the movement of their currencies within the EMS band, or to repurchase their creditors' currencies for the purpose of settling debts arising from previous intervention operations. Up to the present, such intra-marginal intervention has been entirely dependent upon the consent of the central bank issuing the intervention currency. This is why, in practice, some countries wishing to intervene before their fluctuation limits have been reached prefer using dollars because, in an emergency, they cannot make immediate and automatic use of Community currencies. This practice can have undesirable effects to the extent it reinforces a given trend of the dollar.

Although important, this intervention was far from exhausting the system's resources. No calls were made on the short-term monetary support facility nor on medium-term financial assistance. But, it should be added, it was also the possibility of obtaining uncondi-

---

[6] See Chapter 5 of the *Annual Economic Review* 1981-82, op. cit.
[7] See *Annual Economic Review* 1981-82, op. cit.

tional loans on the international credit market which made it unnecessary to resort to the EMS' conditional credit mechanisms.

Interestingly, this degree of intervention has not, generally speaking, resulted in the build-up of large debtor or creditor positions with the FECOM. 'Italy, Ireland and the Netherlands have practically never had a net ECU position; and when they have, it has been a very low percentage of the ECU that they received through the swap operations. Germany's net position has changed from being positive to negative and then positive again, but at the maximum reached 4% of its ECU holdings. Denmark and Belgium have consistently had substantial net negative positions, and France has had a net positive position. The total of the negative or positive positions has reached 8% of the quantity of ECU created through the swap arrangements.' [8]

This experience of positions with the FECOM seems to indicate that member countries have largely observed the rules of the system, by adapting their internal monetary conditions to the EMS requirements in due time while following a policy of borrowing on the international capital market in order to finance their current account deficit. But it also means that the ECUs received by central banks against their deposits of gold and dollars are still little used as means of settlement, and that the official market of the ECU remains underdeveloped.

(c) The fact that a relative stability of exchange rates could prevail in the EMS, without overly straining the mechanisms of intervention and of monetary support, is due to several factors.

(i) First of all, the system was far less rigid, in both its construction and its operation, than its critics initially claimed. The elements of flexibility built into its mechanisms could alleviate the need for intervention when tensions arose. The maximum permissible spread between two currencies at any one time—which is 2.25%, but 6% when one of the two currencies is the Italian lira—has frequently been exploited. Several currencies, including the Belgian franc more than once, have occupied the bottom of the band without much interruption while the top was held either by the traditionally strong currencies in the system, such as the mark, in 1979 and 1981 or the guilder between September 1982 and March 1983, or by a currency which particular circumstances made momentarily strong, as the French franc in 1980, or by weaker currencies during the period following a realignment, such as the French franc after 5 October 1981 or the Irish pound, the Italian lira and the French franc after 21 March 1983. It should be noted that the Italian lira almost never used up its full 6% margin, the Italian authorities generally stepping in to intervene when a threshold of 3 or 4% was reached.

Moreover, reversals of positions within the currency band can, in a relatively short time, double the maximum spread which is authorized at any one time. Thus between January and May 1981, the French franc moved from the top to the bottom of the band, while the mark followed the opposite course: so the spread between these two currencies reached 4.5% within a fairly short span of time without need for a parity adjustment.

---

[8] See 'Documents relating to the EMS', op. cit. p. 44.

(*ii*) Another element of flexibility lies in the fact that parities in the EMS are 'stable but adjustable'. Central rates can thus be changed by common agreement if the divergence between any two currencies of the system becomes too strong or too persistent to be effectively contained within the authorized margin, by intervention or by interest rate differentials.

Seven readjustments of the central rates have occurred so far. A common feature of these operations was the calmness and the swiftness with which they were carried out, possibly reflecting a greater willingness on the part of the system's member countries to accept limited adjustments when they seemed necessary, instead of accumulating delays as happened too often under the Bretton Woods regime.

TABLE IV - 5

Monetary realignments in the EMS: devaluations (−) or revaluations (+)
in % against the other currencies

Currency	24 September 1979	30 November 1979	22 March 1981	5 October 1981	22 Febraury 1982	14 June 1982	21 March 1983
BFR/LFR	0	0	0	0	−8.5	0	+1.5
DKR	−2.9	−4.8	0	0	−3.0	0	+2.5
DM	+2.0	0	0	+5.5	0	+4.25	+5.5
FF	0	0	0	−3.0	0	−5.75	−2.5
IRL	0	0	0	0	0	0	−3.5
LIT	0	0	−6.0	−3.0	0	−2.75	−2.5
HFL	0	0	0	+5.5	0	+4.25	+3.5

TABLE IV - 6

Appreciation or depreciation of bilateral central rates for the currencies participating
in the EMS exchange rate mechanism between 13 March 1979 and 21 March 1983 [1]

Currency	BFR/ LFR	DKR	DM	FF	IRL	LIT	HFL
BFR/LFR	0	+ 1.0	−21.5	+ 4.2	− 3.8	+ 7.4	−18.4
DKR	− 1.0	0	−22.3	+ 3.2	− 4.7	+ 6.4	−19.2
DM	+27.4	+28.7	0	+32.8	+22.6	+36.9	+ 4.0
FF	− 4.0	− 3.1	−24.7	0	− 7.6	+ 3.1	−21.7
IRL	+ 3.9	+ 4.9	−18.5	+ 8.3	0	+11.6	−15.2
LIT	− 6.9	− 6.0	−27.0	− 3.0	−10.4	0	−24.1
HFL	+22.6	+23.8	− 3.8	+27.7	+18.0	+31.7	0

[1] The table is to be read horizontally (for instance the DM appreciated by 27.46% against the BFR, and the latter depreciated by 21.5% against the DM).

The cumulative effect of these readjustments on the bilateral parities and on the ECU-related central rates appears in Table IV-6 and Graph B.

The origin and nature of the tensions that motivated the readjustments varied. The *September 1979* realignment was mainly due to tensions *outside* the system. During the summer of 1979 the dollar began to weaken again after a period of firming up which had followed the support package in the autumn of 1978 in the wake of increasing inflationary

GRAPH B

Development of the exchange rate of the EMS currencies relative to the EMS
(ECU less its sterling component)

Base 100: March 1979 — Monthly averages

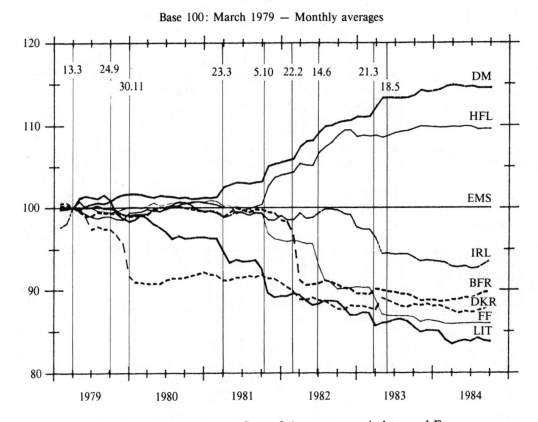

pressures in the United States. The outflow of short-term capital toward Europe gave an upward push to the mark, in a first place forcing the Bundesbank to sell DM 20 000 million in the third quarter of 1979 to contain tensions between the German currency and the EMS weak currencies (at the time the Belgian franc and the Danish krone).

To be sure, these sales of German marks were largely offset in Germany by domestic credit restrictions, in such a way that the statistical data did not register any concomitant acceleration of monetary growth. Nevertheless the Bonn authorities were fearful of the inflationary impact that a prolongation of tensions and of intervention might eventually have. The realignment of 24 September 1979 aimed to bring them to an end by quelling speculation.

The external origin of those tensions was clearly underlined in the statement which the Commission issued on the day of the realignment: 'The adjustment decided on is mainly in response to pressures from outside the system, ... It is therefore perfectly normal. One of the principles of the EMS is that it should be flexible enough to allow changes in positions that favour speculation. The parity changes decided on yesterday are entirely consistent with the structure of the EMS itself.'

82

The new *devaluation of the Danish krone,* decided at the end of *November 1979,* was part of a package of corrective measures adopted by the newly elected government. But it also took its place in the succession of limited adjustments through which Denmark attempted, and to some extent succeeded, in improving its competitiveness and reducing its external deficit, first in the 'snake' and then in the EMS. The krone was thus devalued by 4% in October 1976, 3% in April 1977, 5% in August 1977, 2.9% in September 1979, 4.8% in November 1979 and 3% in February 1982.

The two realignments that occurred in 1981 were, to a greater extent, motivated by *tensions inside the EMS* due to persisting differences in inflation rates. The *devaluation of the lira in March 1981* was a partial adjustment of the exchange rate to the strong rise in relative costs and prices which had taken place in Italy. Between 1978 and 1981 unit labour costs, in national currency, went up at the average annual rate of 17.5% as against 3.9% in Germany. However, in the years prior to the EMS, the depreciation of the lira had more than offset Italy's higher rate of inflation. Therefore it initially had at its disposal a margin which, jointly with the authorized 6% deviation, allowed the first tensions to be absorbed before an adjustment of the central rate became necessary.

The *October 1981 realignment* essentially involved the French franc and the German mark, with the Italian lira and the Dutch guilder respectively following those two currencies.

With this correction France, in the words of the comment issued by its Minister for Finance Mr Jacques Delors, wanted to 'wipe off the past and set the clocks right'. Indeed, the French franc, which had entered the EMS at a slightly undervalued rate and had thus enjoyed at the outset some freedom of manoeuvre, had since been handicapped, relative to the mark, by a distinctly higher inflation rate. The new French Government, prompted by its desire to kick-start growth, rightly wanted to rid itself of this competitive disadvantage by devaluing the franc. However, the operation was not accompanied by domestic restriction, and therefore was not able to prevent an increase of the inflation differential between France and Germany and of the French trade imbalance in the months that followed.

The *realignment of 21 February 1982* requires particular comment. It consisted chiefly of a *devaluation of the Belgian franc* by 8.5%. Denmark saw in this realignment an opportunity to obtain another limited adjustment of her currency, which was devalued by 3%. The size of the change requested by Belgium was surprising or even disturbing to many commentators. But, in fact, the 8.5% change was no different to the rate by which the French franc and the lira had been devalued a few months earlier against the mark and the guilder (though, of course, the Belgian franc was devalued not only against these two currencies but also against the other EMS currencies, except for the krone). Moreover, the Belgian authorities very openly stated their intention of performing a single and once-and-for-all depreciation, rather than the series of limited changes which Denmark has carried out in the EMS and whose combined effect amounts to a devaluation of more than 10%.

Perhaps more surprising was the fact that this adjustment did not seem to be required by the divergence of inflation rates. From the start of the EMS, Belgium had ranked with the Netherlands and Germany among the low-inflation countries in the system. A few months earlier, this record on inflation had been put forward by the Belgian authorities as one of the arguments against a devaluation of the Belgian franc in the October 1981 realignment.

But another type of divergence had developed over the years in the Belgian economy relative to its EMS partners, in the form of a fundamental deterioration in the trend of the price-cost ratio. This largely explained the worsening of Belgium's balance of payments and the endemic weakness of its currency in the EMS. To be sure, by giving prior claim to an exchange rate objective and by upholding the franc's parity, Belgium's strict monetary policy had gained a large measure of success in controlling inflation, since the prices of Belgian products had necessarily to fall into line with those of the main competitors, i.e. Germany and the Netherlands. But, unfortunately, this monetary discipline was not accompanied by a similar dose of discipline in regard to the State's finances and the rate of change of private incomes. Therefore, the relatively low rate of inflation concealed a growing deterioration in corporate profitability (especially in the sector exposed to international competition), a decline in the country's productive capacity through the disappearance of firms, and a drop in industrial employment.

Some have argued that it would have been preferable, and more in keeping with the EMS's objectives, to eliminate this fundamental divergence gradually, by taking internal measures to squeeze costs and reduce deficits. This was the road that previous Belgian governments had in fact tried to take. But their experience had shown how arduous it could be, particularly in a world environment of slow or negative growth, where the stagnation of tax yields shifts the whole burden of cutting public deficits onto expenditure-cutting measures. In view of the size of Belgian deficits, this would have implied a genuine and possibly dangerous deflation. On the contrary the devaluation of the currency, coupled with domestic measures to ensure its effectiveness, allowed an impulse of external demand to offset the initial deflationary impact of internal restrictive measures.

It should be noted that this change in the Belgian franc's parity was part of an overall plan for recovery which also included very strict accompanying measures. These aimed to limit increases in nominal incomes (through, *inter alia*, a temporary scaling-down of the customary indexation mechanisms). The objective was also to reduce the budget deficit and restore balance to social security finances. Complemented with fiscal incentives for investment, these measures were explicitly directed against the severe imbalances that increasingly characterized the Belgian economy and explained the growing divergence of its performance—save on inflation—relative to the European average.

On the evening of 21 February 1982 at the conclusion of difficult negotiations, the EMS proved that it could accommodate this type of adjustment. Though it was fairly novel compared with previous operations, it nevertheless carried conviction that it would strengthen the convergence of the Belgian economy with its partners. This was underlined in the communiqué that emerged from the meeting: 'The agreement reached on the Belgian franc was recognized as part of the measures being taken by the Belgian Government to deal with the structural problems of the Belgian economy. Other Member States wished to express their solidarity with Belgium in this effort, the success of which would contribute to the stability of the EMS as well as to the strengthening in the Community of the Belgian economy.'

Like the October 1981 operation, the *realignment of 12 June 1982* was essentially motivated by growing strains between the French franc and the mark. These were caused by the growing divergence of the two economies in respect to inflation and balance of payments. As in October 1981, the guilder followed the mark, and the lira followed the French franc, but only for part of the way.

However, unlike in October 1981, the June 1982 readjustment signalled a change of direction in the course of French economic policy, leading most observers to see in this realignment not a sign of growing instability in the EMS, but on the contrary the beginning of a better convergence of economic policies in Europe.

The accompanying measures adopted by the French Government closely resembled those which Belgium had taken in February 1982. They also aimed to control more effectively the rate of change of prices and incomes and to curb the deficits in the budget and the social security system. Moreover, the Ministers noted in the June 12 communiqué that the decision to devalue the lira was part of an Italian Government programme to redress public finances and the economy in general.

The countries whose currency was revalued on 12 June, Germany and the Netherlands, noted that this adjustment could 'facilitate policies in their countries helpful to an economic upturn'. A few days afterwards, the Bundesbank began to inject additional liquidity into the German economy. Again, this was a clear case of convergence. The strong-currency countries could afford to release the monetary brakes somewhat, while countries with weaker currencies adopted measures of greater austerity.

This progress toward convergence of the internal economic developments was however not sufficient to forestall a renewal of the pressure on the French franc in the first weeks of 1983. This spell of weakness for the French currency was mostly caused by a deficit on the current account of the balance of payments which remained high (USD 4 000 million for the first quarter of 1983), aggravated by private capital outflows which were made possible by a high rate of domestic credit expansion in 1982.

The French authorities' initial response was to fight those tensions by means of intra-marginal intervention on a large scale, both in dollars and in EMS currencies, which had the effect of transferring onto other currencies of the system, such as the Belgian franc, part of the pressure applying to the French currency. Tensions grew worse following the Christian-Democrats' victory in the German general elections of 6 March, but the fact that municipal elections were being held in France at the same time (the second ballot took place on 13 March) delayed the 'moment of truth'. On Monday 21 March, minutes before the opening of the European Council, a general realignment of central rates was announced.

In terms of trade-weighted effective exchange rates within the EMS, this readjustment implied significant variations for the mark (+ 5,7 %) on the one hand, and for the French franc (− 4,4 %), the lira (− 4,3 %) and the Irish pound (− 5 %) on the other hand. The variation was much smaller for the other currencies.

A few days after the realignment, the French government placed in position a battery of measures designed to exploit the effect of the monetary adjustment fully and to give the final seal to the new course of French economic policy first manifested in the previous realignment. They included fiscal measures, both revenue-raising and expenditure-reducing, aimed at cutting domestic demand by an amount equal to 2% of GDP in order to achieve a rapid reduction in the commercial deficit, as well as a significant tightening of monetary policy.

In addition, the German authorities announced right before the realignment that they were cutting by one point the discount rate of the Bundesbank, and this made a further contribution to restoring the cohesiveness of the EMS. Since then, the substantial reduction of the external deficit and of the rate of inflation which occurred in France, the new progress achieved on a more general plane with regard to convergence among the EMS partners, and lastly the strength of the dollar which helps reduce tensions between their currencies, concurred in making this realignment of 21 March 1983 the last to date.

Thus the EMS has appeared to be more and more the true 'anchorage' of a concerted economic policy, especially after those last three realignments. If the EMS had not existed and if European currencies had been floating against each other, neither Belgium, nor France, nor Italy would have been prompted, to the same extent, to undertake efforts aimed at bringing their respective economic performance closer to the European average. As the Commission emphasized it on the occasion of the fifth anniversary of the EMS: 'Disciplinary effects have resulted from the internal pressures generated by the system. Realignments now provide a privileged opportunity for a thorough examination of national economic policies. Although this practice is not explicitly provided for in the rules governing the EMS, it has become usual since the realignment of February 1982. Earlier realignments had been essentially technical operations; changes in par values since then have been accompanied by back-up programmes in the countries requesting a devaluation of their currencies. In an inflationary environment, this method, although not symmetrical, is consistent with the aim of stability.'[9]

(*iii*) Finally, the operation of the divergence indicator was possibly a third factor in promoting relative exchange rate stability in the EMS, through the acceptance of a common discipline. This device, whose construction was described in detail in the previous chapter, has allowed a standardized appraisal of the extent of each EMS currency's deviation from the average of the system's other currencies.

It is possible, therefore, to identify a more general and more basic divergence than the mere deviation of a currency relative to another currency. The indicator can thus instigate the appropriate reaction from the authorities of the country whose currency crosses its divergence threshold: diversified intervention, but also monetary and budgetary measures, or possibly modification of the central rate.

Of course, the divergence indicator cannot replace movements of the currencies inside the authorized fluctuation margins for the purpose of signalling intervention. Its function is a different one.

As the National Bank of Belgium emphasized in a study: 'The divergence indicator is a dial for analysing the position of a currency on the exchange market, but one which goes

---

[9] 'Five years of monetary cooperation in Europe', op. cit.

beyond the simple observation of a currency's bilateral position *vis-à-vis* every other one or of the distance between this currency and its compulsory intervention limits. Indeed, one should underline that these two critical points—the level at which intervention is required and the divergence threshold—are independent of each other. In other words, a currency may reach its intervention limit without having crossed its divergence threshold, and vice versa; and it is also possible for a currency to reach the two critical points at the same time. In fact, the three situations occurred in succession for the Belgian franc in April-May 1979.'[10]

The divergence indicator has fulfilled its allotted role, particularly during the first three years of the EMS. The upper divergence threshold (pointing to a significant appreciation of a currency relative to the average of the others) has seldom been crossed. (One instance was the mark at the beginning of October 1981, prior to the 4 October realignment.) On the other hand the lower warning limit has been reached and overstepped several times. In the case of the Danish krone (in August-September 1979) and of the Italian lira (in March 1981), the reaction of their respective authorities was a change in the central rate. In the case of the Belgian franc (May to July and September 1979, February-March 1980 and February to April 1981) and the French franc (May 1981), the necessary measures including intervention, an increase in interest rates and a tightening of fiscal policy were all taken to redress the situation. More recently—starting in the fourth quarter of 1983 and until March 1984—the Belgian franc remained for several months under its divergence threshold, but rapid improvement followed the publication by the Belgian government, on 15 March 1984, of a comprehensive plan for reducing the public sector deficit.

Nevertheless, within the exchange rate mechanism, certain *bilateral* exchange relationships—most notably between the French franc and the mark—have in practice been the centre of attention, and the importance of the intervention carried out *within the margins* in order to keep these two currencies near their bilateral central rate may have altered the operation of the divergence indicator and deprived it from part of its meaning. But on the other hand one can say that on numerous occasions, the discipline of the system has had a pre-emptive effect, and policies were adjusted before the divergence became too marked. The disciplinary effect was thus reinforced voluntarily, so it is likely that the volume of intervention was thus reduced.

3. Convergence towards internal stability

(a) The factor which, more than any other, might have helped ensure the stability of exchange rates in the EMS, was a better convergence of the member countries' economic performance towards internal stability. This convergence has not been adequate, at least during the first three years, as shown in Table IV-7 where the main indicators of disequilibrium for the year 1982 are presented. It is surprising that, without such convergence, external stability has not suffered more, or needed greater intervention, or more frequent readjustments, than it actually has.

---

[10] 'Le système monétaire européen', *Bulletin de la Banque nationale de Belgique*, July-August 1979, p. 21.

TABLE IV - 7

**Indicators of disequilibrium and of macroeconomic constraints in 1982
for the countries participating in the EMS exchange rate mechanism**

	Unemployment rate	Inflation rate	Current account balance as % of GDP	Long-term real interest rate	Budget deficit as % of GDP
Belgium	13.1	8.7	− 3.6	4.35	− 11.9
Denmark	9.5	10.1	− 4.2	9.40	− 9.1
FR of Germany	6.8	5.3	+ 0.5	3.49	− 3.5
France	8.8	12.0	− 2.9	3.56	− 2.7
Ireland	12.3	17.2	− 8.3	−0.33	− 16.2
Italy	10.5	16.4	− 1.6	3.81	− 11.9
Luxembourg	1.3	9.4	+38.8	1.10	− 2.0
The Netherlands	11.7	6.0	+ 2.7	4.26	− 6.9

Source: Commission departments.

Indeed, since the start of the EMS, the divergence between member countries' economic performance has remained large, particularly in regard to inflation rates. As a matter of fact, one can even argue that this divergence increased under the EMS, and an examination of the raw data would lend support to such a claim, at least for the EMS's first two years. This is suggested by Table IV-8.

TABLE IV - 8

Divergence of prices and of labour costs in the European Community
(for the 10 Member States)

	Average 1961-1974	1975	1976	1977	1978	1979	1980	1981	1982	1983	1984 (e)	1985 (p)
Consumer price index												
(a)	5.4	13.8	10.8	9.8	7.1	9.0	11.2	10.1	8.8	6.2	5.1	4.2
(b)	0.9	6.4	5.2	5.4	3.7	4.6	6.0	5.2	4.6	4.9	3.6	2.8
GDP deflator												
(a)	5.7	14.9	10.6	9.7	8.4	9.3	10.9	9.2	9.0	6.4	4.7	4.1
(b)	0.8	7.4	5.3	5.5	3.6	5.0	7.0	5.4	5.2	4.9	3.6	2.9
Spread between highest and lowest inflation rate in the EMS (eight countries)	3.2	16.5	14.6	14.5	10.2	11.3	14.9	14.4	11.9	12.2	8.0	5.0
Nominal unit labour cost												
(a)	6.0	18.5	8.2	9.0	7.8	8.4	11.9	9.8	7.7	5.8	3.7	2.9
(b)	0.9	9.5	4.9	5.7	4.1	4.8	6.6	6.6	5.8	6.4	4.1	3.3

(a) Average annual rate of growth in %.
(b) Standard deviation.
(e) Estimate.
(p) Provisional.
Source: 'Annual Economic Review 1982-83' in *European Economy,* No 14, November 1982.

(*b*) Following the trough of 1978, the mean as well as the measures of dispersion of inflation rates suddenly go up again in 1979 and 1980, before undergoing a new decline. A similar trend applies to nominal unit labour costs. Nevertheless, this appraisal of the raw data must be qualified.

First of all, it may not be appropriate to compare the period 1979-80 with the immediately preceding years, in view of the strong inflationary impulse set off by the second oil
shock, which roughly coincided with the launching of the EMS. A fairer base of comparison would be the two or three years that followed the first oil shock. [11] Comparing the
years 1979-81 with the years 1974-76, the inflationary surge was on average smaller
during the second period than during the first. In addition, from 1981 on the dispersion
of inflation rates was reduced and, according to forecasts, will be further reduced in 1985,
thus signalling some convergence after the increased divergence of 1979-80, amplified by
the second oil shock. Finally, some convergence appears to have taken place in the
growth of the money stock. A recent study by the Commission shows that the weighted
dispersion among the growth rates of the money stock in the EMS countries went down
from 4.6 in 1979 and 1980 to 4.1 in 1981, 3.3 in 1982, 3.2 in 1983 and 3.1 in 1984. [12]
This evolution seems to reflect the convergence which appeared in the conduct of economic policies in 1982 and 1983, the fight against inflation receiving prior claim in the
countries whose performance on that score had remained unsatisfactory.

(c) Despite these extenuating circumstances, the fact that divergent inflation rates
could initially develop in a system of relatively stable exchange rates without giving rise
to great tensions is surprising. It certainly confounds previous expectations. In such a
system, indeed, one would expect a country whose costs and prices start diverging
upwards from its partners' average to lose competitiveness gradually and therefore to see
downward pressure on its currency.

The EMS mechanisms would then lead this country to the adoption of a stricter monetary policy in order to defend its exchange rate, and this would help stabilize its costs and
prices. Thus, under normal circumstances, the exchange rate mechanism and the associated instruments—in particular the divergence indicator—might have helped bring
about a greater convergence of inflation rates. The increasing divergence that was
observed instead was not due to an improper functioning of the mechanisms, but to a
peculiar combination of external circumstances.

First of all, as we already hinted, in the period that preceded the EMS, countries with
higher inflation on average, such as Italy, had seen their higher rate of price increase
more than offset by the depreciation of their currency, which therefore translated into a
depreciation of their real exchange rate. [13] This was also true for France, Ireland and the
United Kingdom. Those countries (except for the UK, which does not participate in the
exchange rate mechanism) thus entered the EMS with a central rate of their currency that
was relatively favourable from the viewpoint of their competitiveness. In 1981, the
resulting gap was pretty much closed for France and Ireland, while Italy had regained
some of its margin through its devaluation of 6 March 1981. But this permitted France
and Italy to have a relatively favourable balance-of-payments situation in 1979 and still
to some extent in 1980, compared to the system's low-inflation countries with traditionally strong currencies. This is shown in Table IV-9.

---

[11] See Niels Thygesen: 'Are monetary policies and performances converging?', Seminar on European
monetary integration, Copenhagen, 13-14.3.1981.
[12] See *European Economy*, March 1984, Supplement A.
[13] See pp. 75-76 and Table IV-2.

TABLE IV-9
Current Account Balance (a) (% of GDP), Inflation rates (b) and Real Exchange Rates (c) between 1978 and 1982

	1978	1979	1980	1981	1982
Countries with low inflation rates					
Belgium/Luxembourg					
(a)	−1.0	−2.8	−4.2	−4.1	−3.1
(b)	4.5	4.5	6.6	7.6	8.7
(c) (1970=100)	107.7	104.9	100.8	97.8	88.0
The Netherlands					
(a)	−1.1	−1.3	−1.8	+2.0	+2.7
(b)	4.1	4.2	6.5	6.7	5.9
(c) (1970=100)	123.5	120.5	117.9	115.9	120.1
FR of Germany					
(a)	+1.4	−0.8	−1.9	−0.9	+0.5
(b)	2.7	4.1	5.5	5.9	5.3
(c) (1970=100)	109.3	107.8	102.0	98.4	100.4
Countries with high inflation rates					
France					
(a)	+1.5	+0.9	−0.6	−0.8	−2.9
(b)	9.3	10.6	13.5	13.3	12.0
(c) (1970=100)	94.0	96.1	99.3	101.1	97.0
Ireland					
(a)	−4.1	−11.0	−9.8	−12.5	−8.2
(b)	7.2	13.2	18.2	20.4	17.2
(c) (1970=100)	84.8	88.9	93.4	101.0	108.2
Italy					
(a)	+2.4	+1.7	−2.5	−2.3	−1.6
(b)	12.2	14.7	23.0	17.7	16.6
(c) (1970=100)	76.1	78.7	85.9	89.6	92.3

Source: Commission departments.

On the other hand, Germany, which had agreed in 1978 to stimulate its economy for its partners' benefit, and was in addition very dependent upon imported energy sources, experienced the largest external deficit in its history in 1980 (− 11 500 million ECU on current account), which helped weaken the mark in the EMS.

Thus, near the end of 1980, the mark was at its floor against the French franc. The divergence indicator revealed the same relative positions, the mark drawing near its lower threshold and the French franc coming close to its upper threshold.

The paradox in this episode was that the strong-currency country, France, had a rate of inflation which was—and had been for a number of years—more than twice the rate of the weak-currency country, i.e. Germany. Similarly, when the Belgian franc came under speculative attacks in 1979 and in the spring of 1980, the Belgian rate of inflation was among the lowest in the Community. By contrast in 1979 France and Italy, with much higher inflation rates, remained strong in the EMS thanks to their relatively favourable balance-of-payments situation.

This pattern seems to have prevailed in 1980, with the French franc remaining at the top of the EMS for most of the time. The Belgian franc was rather weak. The lira weakened as Italy's external account deteriorated sharply. The mark followed a similar trend for essentially the same reasons, despite Germany's noted performance in internal price stability. In 1981 however this situation began to change, and it sharply turned in 1982. There was a reappearance of a surplus on the German current account, and a strong deterioration of the French balance of payments.

(d) Thus it appears that until 1981 the behaviour of currencies in the EMS was influenced more by a comparison of balance-of-payments performances than by inflation rate differentials. And the fact that the two types of performance did not coincide across countries—at least until 1981—is essentially what explains how the divergence of inflation rates could be maintained and even increased without excessively straining the exchange rates.

An interesting feature of the EMS comes out here, and one that can be considered as a weak point of the system. Viewed as an objective, internal stability is equal in importance to external stability. But when it comes to means and constraints, external stability gets the upper hand, since only by its being threatened is action required under the EMS's operating rules. Thus the EMS promotes the pursuit of internal stability only in so far as it depends upon external stability. When, due to particular circumstances, this bond is untied, at least for a time, as seems to have occurred for France and Italy, then the convergence toward internal stability may have to be given up. Substantial divergences of inflation rates can persist.

As might be expected, this conjunction has been associated with fairly important movements of *real exchange rates* and relative competitive positions in the EMS. Between 1978 and 1982, the relative level of unit labour costs, expressed in a common currency, significantly decreased in Belgium and Denmark. It went up by around 10% in France, 13% in Italy and 25% in Ireland. Of course this could take place because, as we stressed earlier, deviations had occurred in the opposite direction between 1970 and 1978, as Table IV-10 shows.

During the first three years of its existence the EMS to a large extent absorbed the price and relative cost margins which existed in 1978. This gradual resorption could happen precisely because the exchange rate movements allowed by the EMS framework ceased to overcompensate for inflation differentials. The process having been completed, the diverging trends of real exchange rates influenced balance-of-payments behaviour. The countries which continue to have a rate of inflation higher than others must now witness a progressive accumulation of pressures on their currency. Thus, Germany's external imbalance corrected itself in 1981 and above all in 1982, and the mark has now regained its strong-currency position in the system. On the other hand, the lira, followed by the French franc, weakened and had to be devalued. 'Thus, although convergence of inflation rates has still not been achieved (12-month consumer-price inflation rates varied from

TABLE IV - 10

Unit labour costs in common currency
Change in the relative level (*vis-à-vis* the EMS partners)

(1970 = 100)

	1978	1982
Belgium	117,8	99,0
Denmark	102,7	90,3
FR of Germany	99,1	94,6
France	92,6	103,0
Ireland	77,9	103,0
Italy	82,7	95,7
The Netherlands	112,9	112,6
United Kingdom	76,3	117,8

Source: 'Annual Economic Review 1982-83', op. cit.

15.2% in Italy to 2.5% in Germany in July 1983), the EMS has not fully accommodated this, and has exerted a systematic, although not extreme pressure for greater price stability.' [14]

The conclusion one can infer from this investigation is fairly clear. The EMS's performance on convergence toward internal stability has been inadequate, in particular during the first three years. This inadequacy did not seriously threaten the pursuit of external stability at first because of a combination of particular circumstances. But this conjunction could not be maintained. On the contrary, the balance-of-payments relative positions sharply changed in 1982, and the stability of exchange rates in the EMS has been unsettled. Within nine months, from 5 October 1981 to 14 June 1982, three realignments of central rates occurred. They have led to substantial alterations in the bilateral rates. Thus, between these two dates, the official bilateral exchange rates between the mark on the one hand and the French franc, the lira and the Belgian franc on the other were changed respectively by 20.3%, 16.6% and 20.2%. [15]

The persistence of inflation rate differences on a scale such as existed then (from 5 to 17% in 1982) could have provoked new tensions and so jeopardized the pursuit of economic stability. The search for a better convergence toward internal stability was thus in 1982 and still is today a priority for the EMS. But the latest three parity realignments were encouraging in this respect, as we have seen. They have confirmed the EMS's capacity to serve as an anchor for a policy of external and internal stability.

[14] See Annual Economic Review 1983-84, in *European Economy,* November 1983, p. 122.
[15] See Annual Economic Review 1982-83, op. cit.

4. The development of the private ECU [16]

Whereas the 'official' ECUs received by central banks in exchange of their gold and dollar deposits have remained, as we saw, little used, the private utilization of the ECU has been developing fast, particularly since 1982, as private markets replaced, in a fashion, the official authorities to promote its development.

It should be noted however that the mere existence of an official ECU was most probably beneficial to the development of the private ECU. To be sure, much of the attractiveness of the ECU derives from its being a basket of currencies within which fluctuations in exchange rates or in interest rates of the constituent currencies tend to be, in part, mutually offsetting. Therefore the ECU is more stable than other currencies and it offers, against exchange or interest rate variations, some protection which may attract lenders or borrowers, particularly in times of instability. But, in addition, by virtue of the official character of the ECU, this basket of currencies is not just an ordinary basket. Although the utilization of the ECU between central banks still remains completely separated from its private use, the composition of these two types of ECU is identical.

Privately, the ECU is used in particular for:

(i)   public issues of bonds,
(ii) bank loans and deposits,
(iii) the interbank market,
(iv) commercial transactions.

(a) The first *public issue of ECU-denominated bonds* was floated in March 1981 by STET, the Italian public company for telecommunications. The response was such that the amount of the issue had to be raised from 25 to 35 million ECU.

Since then the number of issues has grown at a rising pace. By mid-1984 the total number of issues exceeded 100 for a global amount of more than 7 000 million ECU. The chief borrowers were European institutions (EEC, ECSC, Euratom, European Investment Bank), as well as some national States with balance-of-payments difficulties (France, Italy, Ireland, Denmark). On the investors' side, the market seems to be concentrated mainly in Belgium and Luxembourg.

ECU borrowing takes the form of mostly fixed rate issues with a duration going from three to 15 years, but different formulae have been tried. For instance, there exist ECU-bonds with floating interest rate or with a coupon which is partly a function of the profits made by the issuing company. [17]

The share of the ECU in Eurobond issues thus went up from 1 % in 1981 to 4 % for the first eight months of 1984.

---

[16] Among recent studies focusing on this phenomenon, let us mention: 'EMS, ECU and commercial banking', by Filip Abraham, Jean-Paul Abraham & Yvonne Lacroix-Destrée, in *Revue de la Banque* (Brussels), February 1984. *The future of the EMS and the ECU*, by Robert Triffin. Centre for European Policy Studies, Brussels, 1984.

[17] See 'L'Ecu: future centre de gravité de l'Europe monétaire', in *Bulletin financier de la BBL*, 18 June 1984.

TABLE IV-11

Eurobond issues by currency

(in %)

	SDR	ECU	USD	DM	UKL	Other
1981	1.4	1.0	84.9	4.0	1.6	7.1
1982	0	3.8	85.1	5.0	1.4	4.6
1983	0	4.2	79.2	7.8	3.9	4.7
1984 (first 8 months)	0	4.0	81.1	6.1	4.5	4.3

Source: 'World Financial Markets', *Morgan Trust,* September 1984.

Let us also mention domestic issues linked to the ECU. At the end of 1983 7 such issues had been floated for a total amount equal in value to 3 800 million ECU. The most important borrowers were Italy, Belgium (emprunt Vandeputte) and France.

(b) More than 200 banks in Europe now accept ECU deposits. This development originated in a demand by EEC institutions to open ECU-denominated bank accounts on which interest would be paid in ECU and from which transfers to similar accounts could be made. But nowadays quite a few private companies and individuals have such bank accounts. The bankers' growing interest for such operations and the granting of ECU-loans to their customers gave rise to a genuine structured market which can now absorb any type of loan or deposit operation ranging from very-short to one-year terms.

A counting made by mid-1984 showed that about 30 international bank credits had been granted by then, for a global amount nearing 4 000 million ECU.

(c) More than 200 banks actively take part in an *interbank market in ECU.* Some have issued ECU-denominated certificates of deposit.

A clearing mechanism between banks has been created, in such a way that an interbank transfer in ECU no longer requires either nine different transactions (in each of the constituent currencies) or a preliminary conversion into one currency, thus implying foreign exchange operations. Five commercial banks play an important role in this clearing mechanism, each one having opened reciprocal accounts for ECU-settlements on behalf of the other ones.

A project is currently being discussed, under which the Bank for International Settlements in Basle would play the role of a central clearing institution. [18]

(d) Finally, *companies* can take cover against certain foreign exchange risks by using ECU instruments. Thus, one is not surprised to see some firms use the ECU more and more to cover themselves against the risks attached to financing their exports, particularly those which do mostly business in European Community countries. The Italian

---

[18] See Renaud Ganage, 'La compensation des règlements en Ecu', in *Eurépargne* (Luxembourg), July 1984.

authorities in particular have promoted the use of the ECU for trade transactions, and nearly 12% of Italian foreign trade appears to be now invoiced and paid for in ECU. [19]

Similarly, 'some European multinationals are tending to prefer the ECU to Community currencies and to the dollar for invoicing and even settling transactions with their subsidiaries; by so doing they reduce their exchange risk and simplify their cash management'. [20]

It has also been decided in 1984 to issue ECU credit cards and to create ECU travellers' cheques.

If the private use of the ECU could thus develop in several directions, it is also because the costs associated with ECU transactions could be reduced. As the Commission answered to a question by a member of the European Parliament: 'Until recently the ECU was treated as a basket of nine Community currencies, each of which was the subject of a separate exchange operation, which greatly increased the cost of using this instrument. Two elements have recently allowed to reduce the cost of ECU operations to the cost of foreign exchange operations: first, the monetary authorities of most Member States have by now accepted that the ECU be treated as a foreign currency; moreover, the banking system is gradually setting up an interbank market allowing it to use the ECU as a currency for settlement, thus avoiding its splintering into the component currencies. The costs of subscribing to bond issues in ECU are now the same as for an issue in any foreign currency'.

Nevertheless, there are still official obstacles to the private use of the ECU, particularly in Germany, where the ECU-denomination is considered as an indexation clause. Since such clauses are prohibited by Article 3 of the Monetary Law of 1948, ECU-transactions are forbidden between residents and heavily restricted between non-residents.

Formal or informal recognition of the ECU as a foreign currency by all the EMS member States would end this rather formalistic interpretation of the ECU-denomination.

The quotation of the ECU on the foreign exchange market is a step in that direction. The ECU is now officially quoted at the Paris Stock Exchange (since 4 June 1984) and in Brussels (since 3 September 1984). In addition it is unofficially quoted in Milan and Rome. This quotation is based on supply and demand and thus implies the existence of a genuine market for the ECU. The value given by such a market quotation may, in principle, differ from the one that is computed by the European Commission, which is not based on actual transactions in ECU but results from adding up the official values of the constituent currencies, according to their respective weights in the basket.

Pending the time when the political will to reinforce the official market of the ECU manifests itself, the success of the private market is a reflection of the public's growing desire for a true European currency.

---

[19] *Bulletin financier de la BBL,* op. cit.
[20] Annual Economic Review 1983-84, op. cit., p. 135.

Chapter V — The future of the EMS

1. Towards the institutional phase

(*a*) According to the agreement reached at the European Council in Brussels in December 1978, the EMS was due to enter its institutional phase at most two years after its launch, or in March 1981. This consolidation of the EMS into a permanent structure would have involved, according to the conclusions of the European Council of Bremen, the creation of a European Monetary Fund as well as provision for 'the full utilization of the ECU as a reserve asset and a means of settlement'. The European Monetary Fund was to replace the existing FECOM and represent an important step on the road to European monetary integration. The ultimate goal was to set up a sort of European central bank that would be the crowning achievement in the process of harmonizing the Member States' monetary policies.

This calendar could not be observed. The European Council of Luxembourg in December 1980 decided that the transition to the institutional phase of the EMS would take place 'at the appropriate time'. The postponement can partly be explained by the contingencies of national politics in some Member States. Transition to the institutional phase would indeed have required some modifications of national legislation, and would have implied some explicit transfer of monetary sovereignty. Neither the French nor the German Government wanted this publicly debated at a time when important elections were soon to take place in their respective countries.

Beyond these transitory political circumstances loomed the deeper question as to whether the central banks in some Member States were ready to accept without resistance the transfer of some of their prerogatives to the European Monetary Fund as it was contemplated. No doubt some of them had — and still have today — misgivings about attempts to consolidate the EMS.

Whatever the reasons, the postponement *sine die* of the institutional phase had the unfortunate effect of freezing the EMS within its transitional structures. Every proposal to improve its functioning is bound to be rejected on the grounds that it belongs to an institutional phase which has been postponed by common agreement. This conservative position is often backed up with the claim that the EMS operation has been satisfactory and that there is thus no compelling reason to try to improve it.

But, as we saw in the previous chapter, the relatively good operation of the EMS, in spite of insufficient convergence toward internal stability during its first three years, is due not merely to its intrinsic virtues but also, in part, to a combination of favourable circumstances.

It is worth quoting the opinion of the Bank for International Settlements in its 1982 report: 'The period of reasonable stability of nominal rates until late 1981 was, to a large extent, the product of the weakness of the German mark, with balance-of-payments developments for a time outweighing the influence of inflation differentials. Once the German mark began to strengthen again in the system, after February 1981, it was not long before the divergence of real exchange rates began to create tensions in nominal rate relationships, leading to the realignments that occurred. ... The absence of outside shocks to the stability of the system since March 1979 has reflected the strength of the dollar against the German mark for most of this period. The real test of the system, so far as its susceptibility to outside disturbances is concerned, will only come if there is a renewed and extended period of weakness of the dollar against the German mark.

All in all, the verdict on the working of the EMS exchange rate mechanism during the first three years of its existence may be that for much of the time a weak German balance of payments made reasonable stability of nominal exchange rates possible, despite some marked inflation differentials between the participating countries. For the future, however, stability will have to come from the achievement, and maintenance, of a downward convergence of inflation rates.'[1]

With regard to the fourth and fifth year of the EMS, the BIS' opinion can be supplemented by observing that while definite progress toward downward convergence of inflation rates has been made during this period, an important factor of external stability was the strength of the dollar and the corresponding relative weakness of the EMS strong currencies.

(*b*) The operation of the EMS in its experimental phase has thus shown certain *failings,* given which it seems unthinkable that the *status quo* is a viable long-term strategy. What are these failings?

(*b.1.*) *Not enough convergence toward internal stability,* was, as we have seen, the chief shortcoming of the EMS during its first years. Even if there were extenuating circumstances for such lack of convergence in an international environment that was greatly disturbed, it nevertheless raises serious questions for the EMS's future development. By virtue of the formal mechanisms of the EMS, the pursuit of external stability receives prior claim. It is only when the stability of exchange rates seems threatened, either in movements of the bilateral rates or in the operation of the divergence indicator, that the authorities in charge of the currency or currencies concerned are compelled or presumed to take action. But a divergence of economic performance (other than a divergence of the currency) is not directly penalized under EMS rules. For instance, having an inflation rate higher than the average of the partner countries does not entail any obligation or presumption to act in order to reduce it, at least as long as this does not lead to a weakening of the currency. It is only in an indirect way therefore that the EMS rules foster convergence toward internal stability.

---

[1] *Fifty-second Annual Report,* Bank for International Settlements, Basle, 14.6.1982, p. 152.

(*b.2.*) As we saw earlier (Chapter IV, p. 77), tensions inside the EMS often originate outside it, because an inflow of short-term capital into investments in European currencies does not affect those currencies evenly. The EMS creators were well aware of this problem. It was for this reason that the agreement setting up the EMS also provided for the '*coordination of exchange rate policies* vis-à-vis third countries and, as far as possible, a concertation with the monetary authorities of those countries'. This type of coordination has rather been *neglected* until now, and this is a second failing of the EMS.

However, one can also argue that, to the extent that there is a key currency within the EMS—the German mark— it is in fact the Bundesbank which determines the common policy toward the dollar. The positions of other EMS currencies in relation to the dollar are determined either by the inaction or by the concerted intervention of the Bundesbank and the Federal Reserve Bank. This of course is one of the aspects of the key currency position enjoyed by the mark in the EMS, and it reflects the powerful image of financial stability which Germany offers in the eyes of international investors. If other EMS currencies were equally attractive from the point of view of their financial stability, it is likely that international investors would more equally spread their short-term assets over the European Community, and that occasional flights from or to the dollar would be less massively concentrated on the mark. Thus, in the long run, a better convergence of economic performance within the Community might be conducive to a more balanced common policy toward the dollar.

Meanwhile, the current state of affairs has obvious drawbacks. When the dollar weakens, the flight into the mark can create tensions within the EMS. The Federal Reserve Bank can then help release those tensions by selling marks on the market, using its swap credit line with the Bundesbank to that effect. However, when the dollar has regained some ground, the US authorities have to purchase marks on the market in order to settle their debt with the Bundesbank. They sometimes do it without much regard for the state of exchange rates inside the EMS. A new upsurge of the mark and new tensions can thus arise, tensions that may not bear any objective relation to the basic economic data in the European Community.

At other times, when the mark is not pushed upward by the weakness of the dollar, the use of the mark as the favourite intervention currency by the Federal Reserve Bank can again create tensions in the EMS. Thus for instance, at the beginning of April 1980, interest rates in the United States dropped quickly, and so did the dollar; but at the same time the mark was weak in the EMS in view of the magnitude of Germany's current account deficit. Nevertheless the Federal Reserve Bank started selling marks to support the dollar, thus pushing the mark down to its floor in the EMS and forcing the Bank of France to purchase marks. The Federal Reserve Bank realized its error after a while and thereafter used French francs in limited amounts to intervene in support of the dollar.

But European central banks may sometimes perpetrate the same kind of offence against the US currency by using the dollar too exclusively for their own uncoordinated intervention. Americans have often complained of the dominant use of the dollar for this intervention. Strong, even though unintended, upward or downward pressure on the market rates of the dollar can arise, irrespective of developments in the US balance of payments, simply because European countries' surpluses or deficits switch from eager to reluctant dollar holders, or vice versa.

(*b.3.*) The third failing of the EMS has to do with the conditions under which the FECOM gets reserves from the central banks and *issues ECU* in counterpart. Under the present system, as we have seen in Chapter III, central banks transfer to the FECOM 20% of their gold reserves and 20% of their dollar reserves, in the form of three-month revolving swaps against ECU. There was first an agreement to renew such swaps every third month until 13 March 1983, unless the transition to the institutional phase should occur before that date and generate a new formula for transferring reserves. This agreement was then extended for two years, and will presumably be extended again before the 13 March 1985 deadline, failing which extension the swaps will be dissolved. Each quarterly renewal gives an opportunity to adjust the *volume* of the reserves transferred (to take account of possible changes in central banks' holdings of reserves) and to adjust the *value* of the ECU issue (to take account of variations in the market prices of the assets transferred).

There are serious *drawbacks* attaching to this system:

(i)   First of all, the possibility of having to re-set the system at point zero at the end of the transitional period, by a dissolution of the swap agreements, tends to give the ECU a precarious existence which is not conducive to an extension of its use.

(ii) Secondly, through the quarterly adjustments in the value of the ECU issue, automatic variations in the amount of ECU liquidity can occur on a large scale, especially for the ECU created against gold transfers, while bearing no relation to the member countries' credit needs. Thus, the issue of 23 000 million ECU in March 1979 grew into nearly 50 000 million in April 1981 and fell back to less than 40 000 million in April 1982. [2]

(iii) Finally, the part played by the FECOM is a purely passive one, since it has no controlling power over the amounts of ECU issued nor over the use of the transferred reserves. Not being free to use the reserves against which the ECU are created, the FECOM cannot thus guarantee the convertibility of the ECU. [3]

These drawbacks and restrictions do not seem to be compatible with 'the full utilization of the ECU as a reserve asset and a means of settlement', as the institutional phase of the EMS was foreseen in December 1978.

Moreover, the precarious status and the limited role which thus follow for the ECU may aggravate the difficulties which arise from the fluctuations of the dollar and from the lack of a concerted policy toward it. For if it were possible to extend the role of the ECU as a reserve asset in such a way that it would partly supersede the EMS dominant currencies in this function, this would most probably reduce the tensions between European currencies that originate outside, and make the task of coordinating exchange policies *vis-à-vis* third currencies easier.

---

[2] See Table III-5, p. 69.
[3] See 'Documents relating to the EMS', op. cit. p. 55.

2. Reforms proposed in 1981

Taking notice of these shortcomings, we made a few proposals in 1981 [4] that were aimed at improving the operation of the EMS, pending the advent of its institutional phase. Those proposals bore upon convergence, a possible extension of the role of the FECOM and a broadening of the use of the ECU.

(a) To ensure a better *convergence* of EMS members' economic performances, we proposed first of all that the *existing instruments be used more systematically,* in particular the Commission's prerogative to address specific recommendations to countries which negatively diverge from their partners. This prerogative is based on the Council's decision of 18 February 1974 which referred to 'the achievement of a high degree of convergence among the economic policies of the European Community Member States'. Article 11 of this decision stipulates *inter alia* that when a Member State follows policies, whether economic, monetary or fiscal, which deviate from the guidelines agreed by the Council or which could be hazardous for the Community as a whole, the Commission may address a recommendation to the State concerned. The recommendation directed by the Commission at the Belgian Government on 22 July 1981 was based on this decision.

We suggested moreover that one should investigate the feasibility of setting up a new *indicator for the divergence of inflation rates.* Such an indicator was not intended to replace the present mechanism of the divergence indicator, which prompts member countries to take the necessary measures when their currencies cross the divergence threshold, but rather to introduce a like automatic signal, also paired with a presumption to take action, in order to fight against the divergence of the rates of inflation. This new indicator would flash every time a country's inflation rate started diverging upwards and significantly away from its partners' average.

Of course, a country whose 'inflation indicator' lights up would not be expected to take drastic anti-inflation measures that could yield results at once. But it would at least have to consult with its partners over the measures it had taken or intended to take in order to fight inflation. This would have the effect of making a country's excessive inflation an area of common concern, and no longer simply a problem which can be safely ignored as long as it does not jeopardize external stability within the EMS. [5]

(b) Furthermore we proposed that, without waiting for the creation of the European Monetary Fund specified for the institutional phase of the EMS, the role of the FECOM might be strengthened and broadened by the setting up of a *permanent board of the FECOM.* This could be done without the need at this stage for a preliminary agreement on the structure, competence and mandate that the EMF should have in its final form, as

---

[4] See J. van Ypersele, Unpublished lecture given in Bonn on 17.2.1981, reviewed in *Bulletin de l'Agence Europe,* No 3080 to 3082 (18-20.2.1981). See also J. van Ypersele: 'EMS helps to bring calm out of instability', *Financial Times,* Supplement on Europe, p. V, 7.12.1981.

[5] On 24 May 1984 the European Parliament, following a report by British Member Sir Brandon Rhys Williams, recommended the institution of an *indicator of convergence* on economic developments that, after the fashion of the EMS divergence indicator, would imply action by the Member States and recommendations by the Council when the signals would flash.

was provided by the Bremen conclusions. But it would nevertheless be useful if the foundation of this permanent board were to include a certain number of enabling clauses that would allow it gradually to take up new responsibilities, and that would therefore facilitate the transition to the institutional phase and to the European Monetary Fund when the economic and political conditions were ripe.

As to the responsibilities that this permanent board should exercise, they were, according to our proposals, to cover three fields of action, namely:

(i) *The management of the EMS external reserves and the control of the creation of ECU.* This would imply that transfers of dollars against ECU by the central banks would be made permanent.

(ii) *The management of the very short-term and short-term credit mechanisms.*

(iii) *The coordination of intervention in third currencies,* and particularly in dollars, in the form of a swap credit line between the FECOM and the Federal Reserve Bank, which would totally or partially replace the bilateral swap agreements which exist today between the Federal Reserve Bank and the central banks of EMS member countries.

(*b.1.*) In the present system for transferring reserves to the FECOM there is no room for truly joint management of the EMS's external reserves. The FECOM has no discretionary power over the use of the reserves deposited by central banks, while the ECU issued against these reserves lead a precarious existence. We proposed in consequence to *make the transfers of dollars permanent* (an *ad hoc* formula would be needed for gold, which poses particular problems). Such a consolidation would have important consequences for the EMS:

(i) It would allow for a possible reform of the mechanism of ECU creation, which is now the automatic result of changes in the market values of gold and of the dollar. A FECOM thus acquiring permanent control over a fraction of the member countries' external reserves might become truly responsible for the issuance of ECU and could regulate the process of ECU creation.

(ii) It would permit genuine joint management of the reserves and would give the permanent board of the FECOM a standing and a status to which, under present circumstances, the FECOM could never aspire.

(iii) It would be a first step toward a real sharing of exchange risks, which is, as Robert Triffin emphasized, [6] a necessary prerequisite to the acceptance of concerted policies of interventions in the foreign exchange market, and particularly in the dollar market.

(iv) The management of dollar reserves by the FECOM would make it possible for this institution, at some later stage of its development, to intervene itself on the foreign exchange market in order to manage the float of the ECU against third currencies.

(v) Finally, the permanence of the dollar transfers would evidently give the ECU a less precarious existence and would therefore remove a big obstacle that now stands in the way of an extension of its use.

---

[6] R. Triffin, concluding remarks at the Seminar on European monetary integration, Copenhagen, 13 and 14.3.1981.

(*b.2.*) The existing systems, set up at different times and possibly rather *ad hoc*, of *very short-term and of short-term credit facilities* for EMS members should be simplified and *managed under the responsibility of the FECOM's permanent board.* This would in fact only carry out the mandate given to the FECOM by Article 3 of the April 1973 founding regulation. This article, indeed, entrusts the FECOM with the 'management of the very short-term financing ... and of the short-term monetary support'. But one cannot hide the fact that the current Community credit mechanisms give little importance to the role of the FECOM. For the very short-term mechanism, its intermediation is necessary in cooperation that is essentially bilateral, but this is a formal construction without any real significance, and the role of the FECOM is in fact restricted to accounting.

Moving to a system in which the FECOM would become effectively responsible for the management of Community credit mechanisms would in fact correspond to a multilateralization of these mechanisms. The existing network of bilateral links which transit through the FECOM would be replaced by a Community institution which, under its own responsibility, would grant a more or less broad array of types of credit, according to the option chosen.

While it would do no more than carry into effect a mandate already given to the FECOM by the existing legal framework, the consolidation of the very short-term and short-term mechanisms under the FECOM's responsibility might open the way to future developments—for instance to a 'communization' of Community credits—whose implications would be fully worked out in the institutional phase. [7]

(*b.3.*) The permanent board of the FECOM should also be given the *task of coordinating intervention in third currencies,* and in particular of improving the coordination of policies toward the dollar. We have already discussed the drawbacks that the lack of coordination has at times entailed.

The growing volatility of the dollar since 1980 has only made the problem more pressing, particularly since the US authorities decided, in the spring of 1981, to refrain from intervening on the foreign exchange market save in exceptional circumstances.

The authorities on both sides of the Atlantic should thus give a clear signal that they care about the volatility of the dollar and that they are bent on reducing it. One way they could give such a signal while reinforcing policy coordination within the EMS would be to set up a swap credit line between the Federal Reserve Bank (FED) and the FECOM in order to replace the existing bilateral swaps. This FED-FECOM swap arrangement could be used in such a way as to stabilize the exchange market within the EMS instead of causing tensions, to the extent that the currency used by the FED to reimburse the FECOM would not need to be the same as the one borrowed for intervention.

The proposed mechanism can be envisaged with the following example: suppose the FED draws on its credit line with the FECOM and borrows a certain amount of ECU. It then requests the FECOM to convert the ECU into German marks, in order to intervene on the market, and the FECOM borrows the marks from the Bundesbank: at this stage, the FECOM would be a creditor of the FED in ECU and a debtor of the Bundesbank in marks.

---

[7] See 'Documents relating to the EMS', op. cit. p. 49.

103

In a second stage, when the time for reimbursing the FECOM had come, the FED would consult its European partners, and for instance might notice the strength of the mark and the relative weakness of the Belgian franc. It would then purchase Belgian francs to reimburse the FECOM. The FECOM would end up being a creditor of Belgium's National Bank and a debtor of the Bundesbank, a situation not unlike the one that might result from activating the very short-term credit mechanism in the EMS.

With this type of mechanism operating to manage the relationship between the dollar and the ECU, the EMS monetary authorities could also try to adopt, together with the United States, a more active policy toward the dollar. This policy would involve sharing a common view on a target zone or a 'zone of probability' for the dollar/ECU rate. The monetary authorities on either side of the Atlantic might then take whatever measures would be necessary for staying within that zone. The target zone, however, could be modified at regular intervals and in no way would imply the automatic defence of a fixed rate for the dollar. [8] Later on, a similar kind of exercise could be considered for the yen/ECU rate.

However, one has to be aware of the fact that, given the type of non-intervention policy being followed in the United States since a few years ago, as well as their monetary policy *stricto sensu,* a more stable exchange rate between the ECU and the dollar would imply either greater fluctuations of interest rates in Europe or a very substantial use of official reserves.

Of course, different European countries are likely to react differently on this particular issue. Depending upon the importance of their foreign trade invoiced in dollars, some countries will be more sensitive than others to a change in the value of the dollar, and will therefore have a different view of the trade-off between the fluctuation of the dollar/ECU exchange rate and the fluctuation of domestic interest rates. Thus the definition of an appropriate common policy toward the dollar cannot be dissociated from the macroeconomic objectives being pursued, nor from the degree of convergence which is achieved when striving for those objectives.

(c) Finally, we suggested in 1981 that the extension of the FECOM's responsibilities in the three areas outlined above should be accompanied by an *enlargement of the role of the ECU,* both in its official functions and in its private use.

(c.1.) If the ECU is one day to be fully used as a reserve asset and as a means of settlement between the EMS central banks, a start must be made by removing, totally or in steps, the existing limits on its acceptability for settlements between central banks. Under the present arrangements, when a member country intervenes at the margin and uses the very short-term credit facilities for that purpose, its debt will be denominated in ECU. If the debt is repaid before maturity, the creditor's currency can be used to that effect. If the debt is repaid at maturity, ECU is normally used, but the creditor has no obligation to accept a settlement in ECU for more than 50% of his claim. In the case of intra-marginal intervention, the debtor has no automatic access to the very short-term credit facilities, but with his creditor's agreement he can be granted such access, in which case the rules for settlement just mentioned applies.

---

[8] See 'Documents relating to the EMS', op. cit. p. 49.

In the EMS's institutional phase, it is clear that all the debts and claims between EMS central banks are to be denominated and settled in ECU. Meanwhile, one could change the 50% acceptability limit, either by dropping it entirely, or by specifying a less restrictive limit, such as, for instance, total acceptance up to the point where a central bank would hold a definite proportion of its reserves in ECU. One could also extend the very short-term credit facilities to the case of intra-marginal intervention when this is carried out after the crossing of the divergence threshold, which case would also give rise to settlements in ECU.

(c.2.) Another direction in which we suggested in 1981 to enlarge the role of the ECU is its private use. In particular we recommended the issuing of ECU-denominated bonds or of bonds securing a reimbursement in ECU, the issuing by commercial banks of certificates of deposit denominated in ECU, and the setting up by the private sector of a clearing mechanism for settlements in ECU. As we saw at the end of the preceding chapter, such an enlargement of the private utilization of the ECU has indeed occurred since 1981 in a very heartening fashion.

Making the ECU more acceptable implies that national regulations regarding its use should be scrutinized so as to eliminate any discrimination which at present exists against this type of currency as compared to other denominations such as the dollar.

Such promotion of the ECU for private use does not only enhance its potential status as a reserve asset, but it may also usefully complement the pursuit of other goals by the EMS. By offering the ECU as a suitable alternative to the mark or to another national currency for the purpose of reserve diversification by dollar holders, it may help reduce the potential strains that exist in the EMS whenever there is a massive conversion of dollars into a European currency or vice versa. Besides, a more extended use of the ECU for the invoicing of international trade and for the granting of associated credits would be of a kind to decrease Europe's vulnerability to the inflationary impact of a rising dollar.

Finally, it should be noted that the possible success of the ECU in progressively superseding European national currencies for diversification purposes and for helping solve the dollar 'overhang' problem will depend on the successful attainment of other important EMS objectives. For as long as there are national currencies which seem likely to appreciate relative to the ECU, it will have difficulties in gaining ground on the financial markets. Thus the convergence of inflation rates and of economic performances within the EMS is also a condition for a growing acceptance of the ECU as a reserve asset.

3. Reforms proposed and discussed in 1982 and 1983

(a) The proposals we made in a private capacity in 1981, though they were not in the least revolutionary, would have meant an important step forward for the EMS had they been adopted. We were of course well aware of the obstacles that stood in the way of adopting some of them, and particularly those that aimed at strengthening the FECOM and enlarging its responsibilities. Considering the latter proposals, we argued that it was not necessary that the responsibilities we recommended investing in the FECOM should be transferred to the board of the FECOM all at once, given that some of those transfers might require important institutional changes and thus need more time. For instance, it rapidly became obvious that a permanent transfer of foreign exchange reserves to the FECOM would imply a procedure of parliamentary approval, and thus properly belonged to the institutional stage of the EMS. [9] Moreover, any move toward an important institutional change that was not preceded by significant progress on convergence continued to meet the most express reservations, particularly within the Committee of the Governors of the Central Banks.

Nevertheless, the political will to proceed with the EMS continued to be present. The European Council of London at the end of 1981, although largely preoccupied with other business (more particularly the problems of the common agricultural policy and of the British contribution to the Community budget), expressed the wish for the Community to enter into 'a closer monetary cooperation between Member States' and to 'commit itself to seeking organized monetary cooperation with its main partners'. It noted that 'the next meeting of the European Council will take place after the EMS has been in operation for three years: at that meeting the Commission wishes the European Council to review the system and outline its future prospects.' [10]

On 14 December 1981, the Economic and Financial Affairs Council reached two conclusions regarding the proposals to be made to the European Council on the development of the EMS. On the one hand, it was not possible as yet to set a date on the transition to the institutional phase, and in particular the creation of a European Monetary Fund as well as the permanent transfer of reserves to that Fund. On the other hand, significant improvements to the EMS and its operation were nevertheless feasible and were to be investigated by the Commission in connection with the Monetary Committee and the Committee of Governors.

(b) The Economic and Financial Affairs Council of 15 February 1982, under Belgian presidency, was entirely devoted to the EMS. The discussion revealed that technical improvements were indeed possible within the existing institutional framework, but that a strengthening of convergence took precedence. It also witnessed the usual split between those for whom the attainment of better convergence must precede any significant reinforcement of the EMS, and those who hope that strengthening the EMS will facilitate the efforts toward more convergence. In conclusion the Council expressed the opinion that measures for developing the EMS should cover four areas, and it noted the Commission's intention to put forward specific proposals. The four areas listed by the Commission and approved by the Council were the following:

(i) *improving the system's mechanisms:* acceptance limit and conditions of ECU creation, means of intra-marginal intervention;

---

[9] See statement by Mr Jean-Yves Haberer, Chairman of the Monetary Committee, to the Economic and Financial Affairs Council of 14.12.1981 on the European Monetary System. See 'Documents relating to the EMS', *European Economy*, No 12, July 1982, pp. 77 and 78.
[10] See *Bulletin de l'Agence Europe*, 4.12.1981, p. 5.

(ii) *opening up the EMS to outsiders:* conditions for holding ECU by institutions outside the Community; efforts to stabilize the relations between the ECU and third currencies;

(iii) *promoting the private use of the ECU:* encouraging European institutions to issue ECU-denominated bonds, removing national impediments to private issues denominated in ECU;

(iv) *reinforcing convergence:* coordination of economic policies, active use of the Commission's prerogatives to send recommendations of economic policy and to follow them through. [11]

The Commission then developed a draft resolution and a communication which were submitted to the 15 March Council. [12] In its preamble the Commission noted: 'the successes attributable to the EMS are fragile, and the object of the Commission proposals is to strengthen and consolidate the system from within so that its contribution to stability and its ability to resist outside shocks are increased... (These) proposals respect the existing institutional framework and form a balanced whole, both from the viewpoint of creditors' and debtors' rights and obligations, and of the elements of solidarity and strictness on which the system has been based. Further, as demonstrated by the work undertaken in close consultation with the competent committees, their adoption is technically possible.'

The 1982 *Commission proposals* covered *four areas:*

(i) the creation and use of ECU in the system;

(ii) the private use of ECU;

(iii) the strengthening of convergence;

(iv) the external relations of the system.

(b.1.) *The creation and use of ECU in the system.* — To avoid the drawbacks associated, in the present system of ECU creation, with the automatic changes which, at each quarterly swap renewal, result from the variations in the price of gold or the market rate of the dollar, the Commission proposed that the creation of ECU be brought under control by retaining the same volume adjustments (i.e. those taking into account the variations in central banks' holdings of gold and of dollar reserves), but by applying the value adjustments to the quantities of gold and dollars transferred to the FECOM by the central banks instead of to the outstanding amount of ECU issued. Thus the quantity of reserves transferred by a central bank at each swap renewal would be inversely related to past changes in the prices of gold and of the dollar, so as to keep constant (or in a constant proportion to the volume of the bank's reserve holdings) the volume of ECU issued. [13]

---

[11] See conclusions of the Council of 15.2.1982.

[12] Commission communication to the Economic and Financial Affairs Council of 15.3.1982 on the development of the European Monetary System and draft resolution on the development of the European Monetary System, in 'Documents relating to the EMS', op. cit., Annex D and Chapter VI.

[13] A possible but less satisfactory alternative, according to the Commission, would be to lengthen from six months to two years the reference period used to calculate the average gold price: this would dampen the effects of erratic gold price movements on the creation of ECU, but it would give rise to a difference between the price of gold on the market and the reference price in the system.

This reform would eliminate the inflationary danger which is involved in the present method of ECU creation, and it would thus encourage its use. With the latter goal in mind, the Commission proposed to abolish the ECU's acceptance limit (which is 50% in the present system) but its counterpart was to authorize central banks to mobilize a net ECU credit position when it is in excess of 50% of their allocation.

(*b.2.*) *Private use of the ECU.* — To promote and to monitor the development of the private use of the ECU, the following recommendations were made:

(i)   to define a sort of 'ECU trade mark' so that the term and the instrument ECU would be correctly used by the markets;

(ii) to remove the discrimination applied to the ECU in national regulations (being neither a national nor a foreign currency, it is subject to any restriction applying to either) by giving ECU the status of a foreign currency in all Member States;

(iii) to promote the widest possible use of the ECU for the accounting, borrowing and lending operations of the Community institutions and of the European Investment Bank;

(iv) to entrust the FECOM with the power to monitor ECU operations and issues by Community institutions as well as by the private sector.

(*b.3.*) *Measures aimed at strengthening convergence.* — In this area, the Commission essentially proposed to activate mutual consultation about policies in the following directions:

(i)   Member States' economic policies would be assessed by reference to a set of *comparative indicators* and to objectives laid down by common agreement. When significant divergence developed for a Member State, the Commission would make full use of the existing consultation and recommendation procedures;

(ii) at regular intervals the Economic and Financial Affairs Council would discuss the national intermediate monetary policy targets and the level of interest rates in Community countries;

(iii) a mutual information and monitoring procedure on the balance-of-payments situation and the external indebtedness of the Member States would be established.

(*b.4.*) *Organization of the system's external relations.* — On this last point, five lines of action were proposed by the Commission:

(i)   to organize *regular consultation,* on monetary problems of common interest, between the Community bodies and the *US and Japanese authorities.* These consultations should also take place at the request of one the parties when a situation out of line with underlying economic data developed on the foreign exchange market, or when interest rate differentials caused excessive and undesirable strains on the Community's money and financial markets;

(ii) to set up meaningful cooperation on matters of exchange rates and interest rates with the United States and Japan, by inviting the US authorities to rescind their decision not to intervene on the foreign exchange market, and by starting discussions on how to establish a *single credit line between the Federal Reserve Bank and the FECOM;*

(iii) to improve the *coordination of Community central banks' intervention in third currencies;*

(iv) to organize the *use of Community currencies* (with access to the very short-term financing) for *intra-marginal intervention,* when a currency crosses its divergence threshold or when its bilateral rate *vis-à-vis* another participating currency deviates by more than 85% of the authorized margin. However, the central banks issuing the currencies used for intervention would have the right to suspend the continued use of their currencies if this obstructed the conduct of their domestic monetary policy;

(v) to open the EMS to third countries, by authorizing central banks of countries which seek to have special ties with the European Community to acquire ECU, either from the participating central banks or by bringing reserves to the FECOM. The Bremen European Council had already provided in 1978 that 'non-member countries with particularly strong economic and financial ties with the Community may become associate members of the system'.

Such were, in brief, the Commission's proposals for developing the EMS. The proposed measures were to form, according to the Commission, 'a necessary and realistic step towards the institutional and final phase, which is still the ultimate objective of the European monetary edifice'.

(c) At the Economic and Financial Affairs Council of 15 March 1982, these proposals were given strong support by the Belgian presidency and by certain countries, France and Italy in particular. However, they could not overcome other countries' reservations or the doubts of the Committee of the Governors of the Central Banks whose chairman said that 'the strengthening of convergence is a prerequisite for any significant future development of the EMS' and that 'technical improvements to particular elements of the system cannot be regarded as a viable alternative to closer convergence of economic policies'.

The Council was nevertheless able to reach a political agreement on numerous points, for example on some suggestions of the Commission in regard to the private use of the ECU, the measures for strengthening convergence and the organization of the EMS's external relations. But it failed to agree on the *technical improvements* to the system proposed by the Commission (i.e. the reform of the mechanism for ECU creation, the raising of the acceptance limit for the ECU, the extension of the use of Community currencies—with access to the very short-term credit facilities—to the case of intra-marginal intervention operated under certain conditions, and the possibility for central banks outside the EMS to hold ECU).

The German monetary authorities took an especially guarded attitude toward these technical improvements, and their reasons were made very explicit in the Bundesbank's *Annual Report* which came out a month afterwards. According to the Bundesbank, the elimination of the 50% acceptance limit 'should only be considered if, within the context of institutional arrangements for the future European Monetary Fund, the unrestricted use of accumulated ECU balances, i.e. their convertibility into other reserve assets, is assured. Since ECU balances represent monetary reserves that can be used only regionally, this would be the only way of making sure that, in the light of the special role of the German mark as an international investment and reserve currency, liquidity needs as well as the largely unrestricted usability of monetary reserves would be guaranteed.' [14] But the current state of non-convertibility of the ECU is the consequence, as we saw earlier, of its precarious means of creation.

As to the possibility of using Community currencies for intra-marginal intervention, it must continue to depend, according to the Bundesbank, on the agreement of the central bank whose currency is being used no matter where the amounts being used come from (own reserves, foreign borrowing, or resort to the very short-term credit facilities). 'If this were not the case, the scope for monetary policy decision-making open to individual central banks whose currencies are chiefly used for such interventions could be excessively restricted; it is limited in any case through membership of the EMS.'

Even if one does not share the view of those who currently oppose a technical reinforcement of the EMS, it is important to understand clearly the logic behind their opposition. The fears they entertain can be summarized as follows. Without a sufficient convergence of the economic results, tensions will intermittently recur between the strong and the weak currencies of the EMS. Though a readjustment of parities can momentarily remove these tensions, too frequent a recourse to this solution might increasingly threaten the external stability of the EMS. The persistence of divergences and tensions would thus give rise to operations of support for the weak currencies.

In the present system, the currencies used for supporting the weak currencies are, generally speaking, either the dollar for the intra-marginal interventions, or the system's strong currencies for the interventions performed at the margins. Extending to certain types of intra-marginal intervention the conditions for intervention at the margins would thus imply, practically, that the strong-currency central banks might have to lend their currencies to the weak-currency central banks in larger amounts than they do now, and therefore might be led to increase their money supply beyond what they deem desirable for their own monetary policy.

Moreover, given that the credit associated with such intervention may be reimbursed in ECU up to a certain proportion (which would be increased further if the acceptance limit were effectively raised) the central banks of strong-currency countries fear that they might be led to accumulate ECU in their reserves and bear an exchange risk greater than they want.

All such dangers would clearly be eliminated, or in any case much reduced, if there were better convergence between the European economies and if, as a result, the distinction between strong and weak currencies became a more fleeting and more contingent one. Lacking such convergence, the usually better performance of the German economy will continue to make the mark the strong currency and normally make the Bundesbank a creditor central bank in the EMS. That the Bundesbank keeps insisting on convergence as a prerequisite for a tightening of bonds in the EMS needs no further explanation.

(d) The first half of 1982 ended with no agreement in sight on reinforcing the EMS. The hopes once entertained by the Belgian presidency of celebrating the EMS's third anniversary with a show of significant progress did not materialize. The European Coun-

---

[14] See *Geschäftsbericht der Deutschen Bundesbank für das Jahr 1981*, p. 84.

cil of Brussels at the end of March 1982 could only reaffirm its hope that progress would take place at some future date. The Council stated that the EMS had functioned satisfactorily during its first three years and should be given a new impulse by strengthening economic convergence, the mechanisms of the system, the role of the ECU, and monetary cooperation between the Community and third countries. [15]

The lack of institutional progress did not prevent the EMS from increasingly asserting itself over the last two years. The chief impulse it received derived not from a reinforcement of its mechanisms, over which agreement has not been reached yet, but from the growing demonstration it made, with its provisional and imperfect mechanisms, that it was useful and even necessary to the European construction.

The external stability which the EMS has brought to European currencies is an advantage recognized by everyone. At a time when the drawbacks resulting from erratic fluctuations in exchange rates are increasingly clear while the possibility of becoming autonomous by letting one's currency float has proved illusory in most cases, the member countries' attachment to the zone of monetary stability which the EMS has brought about is not likely to be seriously questioned.

Moreover, on the occasion of the last three realignments, and quite convincingly on the occasion of the last realignment to date, the EMS appeared more and more as the anchor of a concerted economic policy. The discipline it enforces via exchange rates, and the mutual consultation which is implied by its proper functioning, have the effect not only of coordinating more effectively the Member States' monetary policies, but also, to a growing extent, of bringing their fiscal strategies and their attempts to control the change in private incomes closer.

In this sense, the creation of the EMS and the largely positive experience of its functioning over five years constitute an irreversible progress on the road toward European monetary integration.

But the reality of this positive experience does not imply one should be content with the postponement of reforms. The March 1982 proposals made by the Commission are still with us, as it reminded on the occasion of the EMS's fifth anniversary:

'On the whole, the mechanisms have worked satisfactorily even if they have not been used in practice in exactly the way intended. But this general assessment should not be allowed to overshadow the fact that certain aspects of the system's functioning have been less than satisfactory. As a reserve asset, the ECU is very much a second-class instrument; intra-marginal interventions and their financing lack transparency. The indicator of divergence has shown itself to be deficient. The scope of the system remains limited, something which has implications for its internal equilibrium, its solidity and its external aspects. As regards all these points, the review is broadly similar to that drawn up by the Commission two years ago and on the basis of which it proposed to the Council amendments regarding in particular the official and private use of the ECU and certain mechanisms of the exchange rate system.' [16]

---

[15] See conclusions of the presidency on the proceedings of the European Council, Brussels, 29 and 30.3.1982.
[16] See *Five years of monetary cooperation in Europe,* op. cit.

4. The February 1984 Resolution
of the European Parliament

The political will which sustained the EMS experience rapidly found many echoes in the European Parliament. On numerous occasions proposals aimed at reinforcing one aspect of the EMS or the other were brought to light. The European Members' interest in the EMS reached a climax on 16 February 1984 through the adoption of a Resolution on the consolidation and completion of the European Monetary System along the lines of the proposals made by the Commission in March 1982. [17]

The vote on this resolution was prepared by a report of the Belgian Member Fernand Herman to the Economic and Monetary Commission of the European Parliament. In this report Mr Herman observed that, in spite of its failings, the EMS had worked well, thanks to the flexibility of its mechanisms but also to a combination of favourable circumstances which was not guaranteed to repeat itself in the future; therefore he recommended to strengthen and to improve the EMS without waiting for the 'institutional phase'.

More specifically, the Herman Report recommended:

(i)   to improve convergence by setting up a system of 'flashing lights' that would trigger, like the divergence indicator, a presumption of action for the Member States and an obligation to issue warnings for the European Commission ;

(ii) to improve the mechanisms by allowing, up to some ceiling, intra-marginal intervention in Community currencies, and this in order to limit intervention in dollars which may upset relationships between EMS currencies;

(iii) to strengthen the FECOM by giving it a permanent board which would gradually take up new responsibilities;

(iv) to open progressively the system to non-member countries, in particular by authorizing their central banks to acquire ECU;

(v)   to give ECU the status of a foreign currency in all Member States and to adopt the other proposals made by the Commission in regard to the ECU;

(vi) to bring shortly the pound sterling into the exchange rate mechanism, if necessary by granting it the 6% fluctuation margins that apply to the Italian lira.

Adopted by the Economic and Monetary Commission by a vote of twenty to one plus one abstention, the Herman Report was discussed and approved by a nearly unanimous vote at a plenary session of the European Parliament on 16 February 1984.

Conclusion

It remains our conviction that, without waiting for the coming of the institutional phase, a reinforcement of the EMS would in itself be a significant factor in fostering convergence and in structuring the efforts that are being made to that end.

---

[17] See Document in Annex 4.

(a) We believe first of all that the whole list of the technical improvements to be brought to the EMS, in the spirit of the proposals made by the Commission in March 1982 and restated by the European Parliament in February 1984, should be reopened without delay. Compared to what is at stake, the divergence of opinions which prevented reaching an agreement on these proposals are not, on the whole, very important.

(b) Another way to reinforce the EMS, for which we believe the time has come, would be to make the United Kingdom a fully-fledged member of the system by bringing the pound sterling into the exchange rate mechanism. It appears that the objections made in the United Kingdom against joining the exchange mechanism in 1978 are less and less relevant today. Stabilizing the pound *vis-à-vis* the other European currencies would remove many uncertainties that now afflict the trade and investment relatonships between the United Kingdom and the rest of the European Community. In view of the growing economic involvement of the United Kingdom in the EEC, this would be likely to improve the growth and recovery prospects in that country.

Moreover, such a stabilization would give British authorities a firmer framework for the conduct of their macroeconomic policy than the single-minded pursuit of fixed monetary targets has given them these latter years. As the German experience under the EMS has shown, it is possible to find pragmatic ways of combining the pursuit of monetary growth targets with an exchange rate objective. [18] As to the objection that sterling is a petro-currency and, as such, is bound to remain more volatile on the exchange markets than the other European currencies, it could be met by granting the pound the special 6% fluctuation margins that also apply to the Italian lira. [19]

Bringing into the EMS an important currency like the pound sterling would equip it with a strong currency other than the mark for intervention in Community currencies. The system's stability and balance, as well as its capacity to withstand external shocks, would thereby be strengthened.

It is possible that, as the Commission underlined on the occasion of the fifth anniversary of the EMS: 'the absence of the pound sterling from the exchange rate mechanism was probably beneficial for the system at a time when a fundamental change was taking place in United Kingdom economic and monetary policy and when the country had to adjust to its new role as a net oil exporter. Now, however, the absence of sterling and the drachma is a clear sign that Europe as a monetary unit is not coterminous with Europe as an economic unit. But where sterling is concerned, non-participation is particularly significant: it hampers the EMS in achieving its full potential and reduces the Community's weight in discussions on the shape of the international monetary system. Moreover, it has aggravated the polarization of the system around a single reserve currency that now in practice acts as a link between the EMS and the international monetary system. For sterling's inclusion, in view of its importance in international monetary relations, would necessarily have led to a more balanced share out of responsibilities—and heavy responsibilities they are, as experience has shown. The absence of sterling has, moreover,

---

[18] See J. van Ypersele: 'Bilanz und Zukunftsperspektiven des Europäischen Währungssystems', *Integration*, No 2/80, Beilage zur *Europäischen Zeitung*, No 4/80.

[19] See J. van Ypersele: Memorandum on International Monetary Arrangements, House of Commons, Treasury and Civil Service Committee, London, 12.7.1982.

complicated exchange rate management for EMS countries like Ireland with particularly close trading and financial links with the United Kingdom. It has also made association with the EMS a much less attractive proposition for non-Community countries.' [20]

(c) Last but not least, we believe that, while it is important to reinforce the EMS and thus to promote in an indirect way the convergence of participating economies, it matters even more to work directly at improving this convergence of economic performances toward internal stability, in order to achieve one of the European Monetary System's basic aims.

The imperfect attainment of this objective so far did not seriously threaten the pursuit of external stability during the EMS's very first years, as we saw in Chapter IV. But the particular circumstances that prevailed then—mostly the relative weakness of the German balance of payments, compared to the situations of France and Italy—have by now changed.

It is thus necessary for the countries which have either an inflation rate that is still too high, or an important external deficit, or an excessive public sector deficit, to keep striving to reduce these imbalances rapidly. But it is also essential, in order to ensure some symmetry in the effort to converge, that the countries that are successful on these various scores contribute by a gradual loosening of the fiscal and monetary brakes. They can thus help prevent the adjustment efforts required by a good functioning of the EMS from having excessively deflationary consequences for the European economies as a whole and from amplifying the effect of protraction of the world recession that the excessive interest rates of 1981 and 1982 brought about.

In an international climate that remains unstable and threatening, Europe's monetary reinforcement through a development of the EMS and a better coordination of economic policies would allow the Community to keep to its course in the storms still to come.

---

[20] See *Five years of monetary cooperation in Europe,* op. cit.

Annexes

Timetable of events with important monetary implications for the EEC

1957	25 March	Signing in Rome of the Treaty establishing the EEC.
1958	1 January	Entry into force of the EEC Treaty. Start of the common market.
	27 December	Ten European countries restore the convertibility of their currencies as defined in Article VIII of the IMF Articles of Agreement, thereby signalling the demise of the European Payments Union.
	29 December	14.8% devaluation of the French franc.
1961	6 and 7 March	5% revaluation of the German mark and the Dutch guilder.
1962	5 January	Adoption of the IMF proposal concerning borrowings from 10 industrialized countries. Establishment of the arrangements under the General Agreements to Borrow (GAB) (Group of Ten).
	24 October	Commission Memorandum on the Community's action programme during the second stage of the common market.
1964	8 May	Establishment of the Committee of Governors of the Central Banks of the Member States of the EEC.
1967	18 November	14.3% devaluation of the pound sterling.
1969	28 July	First Amendment to the IMF Articles of Agreement (creation of SDRs).
	8 August	11.1% devaluation of the French franc.
	24 October	9.3% revaluation of the German mark.
	1 and 2 December	Conference of the Heads of State or Government in The Hague, at which the idea of economic and monetary union was launched.
1970	1 January	First allocation of SDRs.
	9 February	Agreement setting up a system of short-term monetary support among the central banks of the Member States of the EEC.
1971	22 March	Council decision setting up machinery for medium-term financial assistance. The Council and the representatives of the Governments of the Member States adopted a resolution on the achievement by stages of economic and monetary union in the Community.
	10 May	Floating of the German mark and the Dutch guilder.
	15 August	Announcement by President Nixon of a wage and price freeze, a 10% import surcharge and suspension of dollar convertibility into gold and other reserve assets.
	12 September	Council decision to accord priority to the search for solutions to international monetary problems and solutions to the problem of organizing the system of exchange rates in Europe.
	17 and 18 December	At its meeting at the Smithsonian Institute in Washington, the Group of Ten decided on a currency realignment, including a dollar devaluation.
1972	21 March	The Council and the representatives of the Governments of the Member States adopt a resolution on the attainment by stages of economic and monetary union in the Community.

	24 April	Entry into force of the Basle Agreement establishing the system for the narrowing of the margins of fluctuation between Community currencies: the snake (margins of 2.25%) in the tunnel (plus or minus 2.25%). The countries taking part were Belgium, France, Germany, Italy, Luxembourg and the Netherlands.
	1 May	The pound sterling, the Irish pound and the Danish krone join the snake.
	23 June	The pound sterling and the Irish pound leave the snake.
	27 June	The Danish krone leaves the snake.
	26 July	Setting up of the IMF Committee on the reform of the international monetary system (Committee of Twenty).
	10 October	The Danish krone rejoins the snake.
	27 to 29 November	At their meeting in Washington, the deputy members of the Committee of Twenty begin their work on the reform of the international monetary system.
1973	1 January	Denmark, Ireland and the United Kingdom become members of the EEC.
	13 February	The lira leaves the snake.
	12 March	3% revaluation on the German mark against the EMUA and announcement by the Council of a joint float of EEC currencies within margins of fluctuation of 2.25% against one another, with the exception, that is, of the pound sterling, the Irish pound and the lira, which continue to float independently.
	14 March	The Norwegian krone and the Swedish krona become associate members of the snake.
	3 April	Establishment of the European Monetary Cooperation Fund (EMCF or FECOM).
	29 June	5.5% revaluation of the German mark against the EMUA.
	17 September	5% revaluation of the Dutch guilder against the EMUA.
	October	Oil embargo and oil price increase during the Arab-Israeli war.
	16 November	5% revaluation of the Norwegian krone against the EMUA.
1974	17 and 18 January	Decision by the Committee of Twenty, at its meeting in Rome, to adopt a gradualist approach to the reform of the international monetary system.
	19 January	The French franc leaves the snake.
	14 June	Publication by the Committee of Twenty of a plan for reform, including 'immediate measures' and completion of its work.
	3 October	First meeting of the new IMF Interim Committee.
1975	21 April	Introduction of the European unit of account (EUA) in certain areas of Community activity.
	10 July	The French franc rejoins the snake.
1976	7 and 8 January	Meeting of the Interim Committee in Jamaica. Approval in principle of the Second Amendment to the IMF Articles of Agreement.
	15 March	The French franc again leaves the snake.
	17 October	'Frankfurt realignment' of exchange rates against the EMUA, with the German mark being revalued by 2%, the Danish krone being devalued by 4%, and the Norwegian krone and Swedish krona being devalued by 1%.
1977	1 April	6% devaluation of the Swedish krona and 3% devaluation of both the Danish and the Norwegian krone against the EMUA.
	28 August	The Swedish krona leaves the snake; 5% devaluation of both the Danish and the Norwegian krone against the EMUA.
	17 November	Commission communication to the Council of 17 November 1977 on the prospect of economic and monetary union.

1978	13 February	8% devaluation of the Norwegian krone against the EMUA.
	1 April	Entry into force of the Second Amendment to the IMF Articles of Agreement.
	7 and 8 April	European Council in Copenhagen: agreement in principle on the creation of a zone of monetary stability in Europe.
	6 and 7 July	European Council in Bremen: agreement on the main lines of a European Monetary System.
	17 October	4% revaluation of the German mark and 2% revaluation of both the Dutch guilder and the Belgian franc against the EMUA.
	4 and 5 December	European Council in Brussels: adoption of a resolution on the establishment of the European Monetary System.
	12 December	The Norwegian krone leaves the snake.
	18 December	Adoption by the Council of two regulations, one concerning the ECU and one concerning the EMS.
	21 December	Adoption by the Council of a decision increasing the amounts of medium-term financial assistance.
1979	12 March	European Council in Paris: announcement of the formal introduction of the EMS on 13 March 1979.
	13 March	Signing by the Governors of the Central Banks and by the members of the Board of Governors of the FECOM of instruments relating to the implementation of the EMS (operating procedures and increase in the amounts of short-term monetary support).

119

Acts of foundation of the European Monetary System

DOCUMENT 1 — Extract from the conclusions of the Presidency of the European Council of 6 and 7 July 1978 in Bremen and Annex

2. Monetary Policy

Following the discussion at Copenhagen on 7 April the European Council has discussed the attached scheme for the creation of a closer monetary cooperation (European Monetary System) leading to a zone of monetary stability in Europe, which has been introduced by members of the European Council. The European Council regards such a zone as a highly desirable objective. The European Council envisages a durable and effective scheme. It agreed to instruct the Finance Ministers at their meeting on 24 July to formulate the necessary guidelines for the competent Community bodies to elaborate by 31 October the provisions necessary for the functioning of such a scheme—if necessary by amendment. There will be concurrent studies of the action needed to be taken to strengthen the economies of the less prosperous member countries in the context of such a scheme; such measures will be essential if the zone of monetary stability is to succeed. Decisions can then be taken and commitments made at the European Council meeting on 4 and 5 December.

The Heads of Government of Belgium, Denmark, the Federal Republic of Germany, Luxembourg and the Netherlands state that the 'snake' has not been and is not under discussion. They confirm that it will remain fully intact.

Annex

1. In terms of exchange rate management the European Monetary System (EMS) will be at least as strict as the 'snake'. In the initial stages of its operation and for a limited period of time member countries currently not participating in the snake may opt for somewhat wider margins around central rates. In principle, interventions will be in the currencies of participating countries. Changes in central rates will be subject to mutual consent. Non-member countries with particularly strong economic and financial ties with the Community may become associate members of the system. The European Currency Unit (ECU)[1] will be at the centre of the system; in particular, it will be used as a means of settlement between EEC monetary authorities.

2. An initial supply of ECU (for use among Community central banks) will be created against deposit of US dollars and gold on the one hand (e.g. 20% of the stock currently held by member central banks) and member currencies on the other hand in an amount of a comparable order of magnitude.

The use of ECU created against member currencies will be subject to conditions varying with the amount and the maturity; due account will be given to the need for substantial short-term facilities (up to one year).

3. Participating countries will coordinate their exchange rate policies *vis-à-vis* third countries. To this end they will intensify the consultations in the appropriate bodies and between central banks participating in the scheme. Ways to coordinate dollar interventions should be sought which avoid simultaneous reverse interventions. Central banks buying dollars will deposit a fraction (say 20%) and receive ECU in return; likewise, central banks selling dollars will receive a fraction (say 20%) against ECU.

4. Not later than two years after the start of the scheme, the existing arrangements and institutions will be consolidated in a European Monetary Fund.[2]

5. A system of closer monetary cooperation will only be successful if participating countries pursue policies conducive to greater stability at home and abroad; this applies to the deficit and surplus countries alike.

---

[1] The ECU has the same definition as the European unit of account.
[2] The EMF will take the place of the EMCF (or FECOM).

DOCUMENT 2 — Extract from the conclusions of the Presidency of the European Council of 4 and 5 December 1978 in Brussels

European Monetary System

The European Council agreed, on the basis of the preparatory work of the Council (Economics and Finance Ministers) and of the Monetary Committee and the Committee of the Governors of the Central Banks to set up a European Monetary System as from 1 January 1979.

The purpose of the European Monetary System is to establish a greater measure of monetary stability in the Community. It should be seen as a fundamental component of a more comprehensive strategy aimed at lasting growth with stability, a progressive return to full employment, the harmonization of living standards and the lessening of regional disparities in the Community. The European Monetary System will facilitate the convergence of economic development and give fresh impetus to the process of European Union. The Council expects the European Monetary System to have a stabilizing effect on international economic and monetary relations. It will therefore certainly be in the interests of the industrialized and the developing countries alike. (...)

DOCUMENT 3 — Resolution of the European Council of 5 December 1978 on the establishment of the European Monetary System (EMS) and related matters

A. The European Monetary System

1. INTRODUCTION

1.1 In Bremen we discussed a 'scheme for the creation of closer monetary cooperation leading to a zone of monetary stability in Europe'. We regarded such a zone 'as a highly desirable objective' and envisaged 'a durable and effective scheme'.

1.2 Today, after careful examination of the preparatory work done by the Council and other Community bodies, we are agreed as follows:

A European Monetary System (EMS) will be set up on 1 January 1979.

1.3 We are firmly resolved to ensure the lasting success of the EMS by policies conducive to greater stability at home and abroad for both deficit and surplus countries.

1.4 The following chapters deal primarily with the initial phase of the EMS.

We remain firmly resolved to consolidate, not later than two years after the start of the scheme, into a final system the provisions and procedures thus created. This system will entail the creation of the European Monetary Fund as announced in the conclusions of the European Council meeting at Bremen on 6 and 7 July 1978, as well as the full utilization of the ECU as a reserve asset and a means of settlement. It will be based on adequate legislation at the Community as well as the national level.

2. THE ECU AND ITS FUNCTIONS

2.1 A European currency unit (ECU) will be at the centre of the EMS. The value and the composition of the ECU will be identical with the value of the EUA at the outset of the system.

2.2 The ECU will be used:

(a) as the denominator (*numeraire*) for the exchange rate mechanism;

(b) as the basis for a divergence indicator;

(c) as the denominator for operations in both the intervention and the credit mechanisms;

(d) as a means of settlement between monetary authorities of the European Community.

2.3 The weights of currencies in the ECU will be re-examined and if necessary revised within six months of the entry into force of the system and thereafter every five years or, on request, if the weight of any currency has changed by 25%.

Revisions have to be mutually accepted; they will, by themselves, not modify the external value of the ECU. They will be made in line with underlying economic criteria.

3. THE EXCHANGE RATE AND INTERVENTION MECHANISMS

3.1 Each currency will have an ECU-related central rate. These central rates will be used to establish a grid of bilateral exchange rates.

Around these exchange rates fluctuation margins of $\pm 2.25\%$ will be established. EEC countries with presently floating currencies may opt for wider margins up to $\pm 6\%$ at the outset of the EMS; these margins should be gradually reduced as soon as economic conditions permit.

A Member State which does not participate in the exchange rate mechanism at the outset may participate at a later date.

3.2 Adjustments of central rates will be subject to mutual agreement by a common procedure which will comprise all countries participating in the exchange rate mechanism and the Commission. There will be reciprocal consultation in the Community framework about important decisions concerning exchange rate policy between countries participating and any country not participating in the system.

3.3 In principle, interventions will be made in participating currencies.

3.4 Intervention in participating currencies is compulsory when the intervention points defined by the fluctuation margins are reached.

3.5 An ECU basket formula will be used as an indicator to detect divergences between Community currencies. A 'threshold of divergence' will be fixed at 75% of the maximum spread of divergence for each currency. It will be calculated in such a way as to eliminate the influence of weight on the probability of reaching the threshold.

3.6 When a currency crosses its 'threshold of divergence', this results in a presumption that the authorities concerned will correct this situation by adequate measures, namely:

(a) diversified intervention;

(b) measures of domestic monetary policy;

(c) changes in central rates;

(d) other measures of economic policy.

In case such measures, on account of special circumstances, are not taken, the reasons for this shall be given to the other authorities, especially in the 'concertation between central banks'.

Consultations will, if necessary, then take place in the appropriate Community bodies, including the Council of Ministers.

After six months these provisions shall be reviewed in the light of experience. At that date the questions regarding imbalances accumulated by divergent creditor or debtor countries will be studied as well.

3.7 A very short-term facility of an unlimited amount will be established. Settlements will be made 45 days after the end of the month of intervention with the possibility of prolongation for another three months for amounts limited to the size of debtor quotas in the short-term monetary support.

3.8 To serve as a means of settlement, an initial supply of ECU will be provided by the EMCF against the deposit of 20% of gold and 20% of dollar reserves currently held by central banks.

This operation will take the form of specified, revolving swap arrangements. By periodical review and by an appropriate procedure it will be ensured that each central bank will maintain a deposit of at least 20% of these reserves with the EMCF. A Member State not participating in the exchange rate mechanism may participate in this initial operation on the basis described above.

4. THE CREDIT MECHANISMS

4.1 The existing credit mechanisms with their present rules of application will be maintained for the initial phase of the EMS. They will be consolidated into a single fund in the final phase of the EMS.

4.2 The credit mechanisms will be extended to an amount of 25 000 million ECU of effectively available credit. The distribution of this amount will be as follows:

Short-term monetary support = 14 000 million ECU;

Medium-term financial assistance = 11 000 million ECU.

4.3 The duration of the short-term monetary support will be extended for another three months on the same conditions as the first extension.

4.4 The increase of the medium-term financial assistance will be completed by 30 June 1979. In the meantime, countries which still need national legislation are expected to make their extended medium-term quotas available by an interim financing agreement of the central banks concerned.

5. THIRD COUNTRIES AND INTERNATIONAL ORGANIZATIONS

5.1 The durability of the EMS and its international implications require coordination of exchange rate policies *vis-à-vis* third countries and, as far as possible, a concertation with the monetary authorities of those countries.

123

5.2 European countries with particularly close economic and financial ties with the European Communities may participate in the exchange rate and intervention mechanisms.

Participation will be based upon agreement between central banks; these agreements will be communicated to the Council and the Commission of the European Communities.

5.3 The EMS is and will remain fully compatible with the relevant articles of the IMF Agreement.

6. FURTHER PROCEDURE

6.1 To implement the decisions taken under A., the European Council requests the Council to consider and to take a decision on 18 December 1978 on the following proposals of the Commission;

(a) Council regulation modifying the unit of account used by the EMCF, which introduces the ECU in the operations of the EMCF and defines its composition;

(b) Council regulation permitting the EMCF to receive monetary reserves and to issue ECU to the monetary authorities of the Member States which may use them as a means of settlement;

(c) Council regulation on the impact of the European Monetary System on the common agricultural policy. The European Council considers that the introduction of the EMS should not of itself result in any change in the situation obtaining prior to 1 January 1979 regarding the expression in national currencies of agricultural prices, monetary compensatory amounts and all other amounts fixed for the purposes of the common agricultural policy.

The European Council stresses the importance of henceforth avoiding the creation of permanent MCAs and progressively reducing present MCAs in order to re-establish the unity of prices of the common agricultural policy, giving also due consideration to price policy.

6.2 It requests the Commission to submit in good time a proposal to amend the Council decision of 22 March 1971 on setting up machinery for medium-term financial assistance to enable the Council (Economics and Finance Ministers) to take a decision on such a proposal at their session of 18 December 1978.

6.3 It requests the central banks of Member States to modify their Agreement of 10 April 1972 on the narrowing of margins of fluctuation between the currencies of Member States in accordance with the rules set forth above (see Section 3).

6.4 It requests the central banks of Member States to modify as follows the rules on short-term monetary support by 1 January 1979 at the latest:

(a) The total of debtor quotas available for drawings by the central banks of Member States shall be increased to an aggregate amount of 7 900 million ECU.

(b) The total of creditor quotas made available by the central banks of Member States for financing the debtor quotas shall be increased to an aggregate amount of 15 800 million ECU.

(c) The total of the additional creditor amounts as well as the total of the additional debtor amounts may not exceed 8 800 million ECU.

(d) The duration of credit under the extended short-term monetary support may be prolonged *twice* for a period of three months.

B. Measures designed to strengthen the economies of the less prosperous Member States of the European Monetary System

1. We stress that, within the context of a broadly based strategy aimed at improving the prospects of economic development and based on symmetrical rights and obligations of all participants, the most important concern should be to enhance the convergence of economic policies towards greater stability. We request the Council (Economics and Finance Ministers) to strengthen its procedures for cooperation in order to improve that convergence.

2. We are aware that the convergence of economic policies and of economic performance will not be easy to achieve. Therefore, steps must be taken to strengthen the economic potential of the less prosperous countries of the Community. This is primarily the responsibility of the Member States concerned. Community measures can and should serve a supporting role.

3. The European Council agrees that in the context of the European Monetary System, the following measures in favour of less prosperous Member States effectively and fully participating in the exchange rate and intervention mechanisms will be taken.

3.1 The European Council requests the Community Institutions by the utilization of the new financial instrument and the European Investment Bank to make available for a period of five years loans of up to 1 000 million EUA per year to these countries on special conditions.

3.2 The European Council requests the Commission to submit a proposal to provide interest rate

124

subsidies of 3% for these loans, with the following element: the total cost of this measure, divided into annual tranches of 200 million EUA each over a period of five years, shall not exceed 1 000 million EUA.

3.3 Any less prosperous member country which subsequently effectively and fully participates in the mechanisms would have the right of access to this facility within the financial limits mentioned above. Member States not participating effectively and fully in the mechanisms will not contribute to the financing of the scheme.

3.4 The funds thus provided are to be concentrated on the financing of selected infrastructure projects and programmes, on the understanding that any direct or indirect distortion of the competitive position of specific industries within Member States will have to be avoided.

3.5 The European Council requests the Council (Economics and Finance Ministers) to take a decision on the above-mentioned proposals in time so that the relevant measures can become effective on 1 April 1979 at the latest. There should be a review at the end of the initial phase of the EMS.

4. The European Council requests the Commission to study the relationship between greater convergence in economic performance of the Member States and the utilization of Community instruments, in particular the funds which aim at reducing structural imbalances. The results of these studies will be discussed at the next European Council meeting.

DOCUMENT 4 — Council Regulation (EEC) No 3180/78 of 18 December 1978 changing the value of the unit of account used by the European Monetary Cooperation Fund [3]

The Council of the European Communities,

Having regard to the Treaty establishing the European Economic Community;

Having regard to Council Regulation (EEC) No 907/73 of 3 April 1973 establishing a European Monetary Cooperation Fund, [4] and in particular the last paragraph of Article 5 of the Statutes of the Fund;

[3] OJ L 379, 30.12.1978, p. 1.
[4] OJ L 89, 5.4.1973, p. 2.

Having regard to the proposal from the Commission;

Having regard to the opinion of the Monetary Committee;

Having regard to the opinion of the Board of Governors of the European Monetary Cooperation Fund;

Whereas Regulation (EEC) No 907/73, in Article 5 of the Statutes of the Fund, requires the latter's operations in the currencies of the Member States to be expressed in a European monetary unit of account of a value of 0.88867088 gramme of fine gold;

Whereas this definition no longer conforms with the rules in force in the international monetary system;

Whereas, apart from cases in which the value of the European monetary unit of account is changed automatically, the past paragraph of the said Article 5 provides that any other changes shall be decided on by the Council, acting unanimously on a proposal from the Commission, after consulting the Monetary Committee and the Board of Governors of the Fund;

Whereas the establishment of a new European Monetary System, which was the subject of the resolution of the European Council meeting in Brussels on 4 and 5 December 1978, provides for the use of an 'ECU' defined as a basket of Member States' currencies,

Has adopted this regulation:

Article 1

With effect from 1 January 1979, the Fund's operations shall be expressed in a unit of account known as the ECU which is defined as the sum of the following amounts of the currencies of the Member States;

0.828	German mark,
0.0885	pound sterling,
1.15	Franch francs,
109	Italian lire,
0.286	Dutch guilder,
3.66	Belgian francs,
0.14	Luxembourg franc,
0.217	Danish krone,
0.00759	Irish pound.

Article 2

The Council, acting unanimously on a proposal from the Commission after consulting the Monetary Committee and the Board of Governors of the Fund, shall determine the conditions under which the composition of the ECU may be changed.

Article 3

This Regulation shall enter into force on 1 January 1979.

This Regulation shall be binding in its entirety and directly applicable in all Member States.

Done at Brussels, 18 December 1978.

For the Council

The President

H. Matthöfer

DOCUMENT 5 — Council Regulation (EEC) No 3181/78 of 18 December 1978 relating to the European Monetary System [5]

The Council of the European Communities,

Having regard to the Treaty establishing the European Economic Community, and in particular Article 235 thereof;

Having regard to the proposal from the Commission;

Having regard to the opinion of the European Parliament; [6]

Having regard to the opinion of the Economic and Social Committee; [7]

Whereas the European Council meeting in Brussels adopted, on 5 December 1978, a resolution setting out the arrangements related to the establishment of the European Monetary System which will come into effect from 1 January 1979;

Whereas, in this context, and not later than two years after the start of the system, the existing arrangements and institutions would be merged

into a European Monetary Fund; whereas, in the meantime, responsibility for administering the new monetary system should be entrusted initially to the European Monetary Cooperation Fund, set up by Regulation (EEC) No 907/73; [8]

Whereas, by Regulation (EEC) No 3180/78, the Council adopted the ECU as the unit of account used by the European Monetary Cooperation Fund;

Whereas, for the system to begin functioning, it is necessary to provide immediately for the creation of a supply of ECU against part of the central banks' reserves placed with the system, and for those ECU to be used as a means of settlement within the system;

Whereas, in this context, the introduction of the ECU into the operations of the European Monetary Cooperation Fund and its utilization as a means of settlement are necessary if the objectives pursued by the Community are to be achieved, notably the gradual convergence of Member States' economic policies, the smooth functioning of the common market and the attainment of economic and monetary union; whereas the powers needed to set up the system are not provided for in the Treaty,

Has adopted this regulation:

Article 1

The European Monetary Cooperation Fund is hereby empowered to receive monetary reserves from the monetary authorities of Member States and to issue ECU against such assets.

Article 2

The Fund and the monetary authorities of the Member States are hereby empowered to use ECU as a means of settlement and for transactions between those authorities and the Fund.

Article 3

The Board of Governors of the Fund shall take the administrative measures necessary for the implementation of Articles 1 and 2.

Article 4

This Regulation shall enter into force on 1 January 1979.

[5] OJ L 379, 30.12.1978, p. 2.
[6] OJ C 296, 11.12.1978, p. 62.
[7] Opinion delivered on 29 and 30.11.1978.

[8] OJ L 89, 5.4.1973, p. 2.

This Regulation shall be binding in its entirety and directly applicable in all Member States.

Done at Brussels, 18 December 1978.

For the Council
The President
H. Matthöfer

DOCUMENT 6 — Council Decision of 21 December 1978 amending Decision 71/143/EEC setting up machinery for medium-term financial assistance

(78/1041/EEC)

The Council of the European Communities,

Having regard to the Treaty establishing the European Economic Community, and in particular Articles 103 and 108 thereof,

Having regard to the opinion of the Monetary Committee,

Having regard to the proposal from the Commission,

Whereas the European Council meeting in Brussels adopted, on 5 December 1978, a resolution setting out the arrangements for the establishment of the European Monetary System; whereas this system implies an increase in the commitment ceilings of the Member States within the medium-term financial assistance machinery; whereas the European Council expressly laid down that the amount of this assistance should be raised to 11 000 million ECU effectively available;

Whereas the resolution of the European Council of 5 December 1978 states that the existing credit arrangements will be maintained for the initial phase of the European Monetary System and will be consolidated into a single fund in the final phase; whereas it is appropriate that the obligations of the Member States cover the whole transitional period of the system;

Whereas it is expedient to use the ECU in medium-term financial assistance as well as in short-term monetary support for denominating claims and obligations,

Has adopted this decision:

Article 1

Council Decision 71/143/EEC of 22 March 1971 setting up the machinery for medium-term financial assistance, [9] as last amended by Decision 78/49/EEC, [10] is hereby amended as follows:

1. Article 1 (2) shall read as follows:

   '2. This obligation shall apply until 31 December 1980.

2. The first sentence of Article 3 (5) shall be replaced by the following:

   'The claims and obligations arising from the implementation of mutual assistance shall be expressed in ECU as defined in Article 1 of Regulation (EEC) No 3180/78'. [11]

3. The first sentence of Article 5 (2) shall be replaced by the following:

   'Where refinancing takes place from outside the system, the debtor State shall agree that its debt, originally denominated in ECU, shall be replaced by a debt denominated in the currency used for the refinancing.'

4. The Annex shall read:

   ANNEX

   The ceilings for credits provided for in Article 1 (1) of this decision shall be as follows:

	(million ECU)	*(% of total)*
FR of Germany	3 105	22.02
Belgium	1 000	7.09
Denmark	465	3.30
France	3 105	22.02
Ireland	180	1.28
Italy	2 070	14.68
Luxembourg	35	0.25
Netherlands	1 035	7.34
United Kingdom	3 105	22.02
	14 100	100.00

Article 2

This decision is addressed to the Member States.

The Member States shall complete any necessary internal procedures for the implementation of this decision not later than 30 June 1979. In the mean-

---

[9] OJ L 73, 27.3.1971, p. 15.
[10] OJ L 14, 18.1.1978, p. 14.
[11] See Document 4.

time, Member States which still need national legislation shall make their extended medium-term quotas available by an interim financing.

Done at Brussels, 21 December 1978.

For the Council
The President
Otto Graf Lambsdorff

DOCUMENT 7 — Communication [12] on the calculation [13] of the equivalents of the ECU and of the European unit of account published by the Commission

1. Definition of the ECU and the European unit of account (EUA)

The ECU, as defined in Council Regulation (EEC) No 3180/78 of 18 December 1978 [14] and the EUA, as defined in Article 10 of the Financial Regulation of 21 December 1977 [15] are composed of the same amounts of national currencies.

These amounts are as follows:

0.828	German mark,
1.15	French francs,
0.0885	pound sterling,
109	Italian lire,
0.286	Dutch guilder,
3.66	Belgian francs,
0.140	Luxembourg franc,
0.217	Danish krone,
0.00759	Irish pound.

The equivalent of the ECU and EUA in any currency is equal to the sum of the equivalents of these amounts in that currency.

2. Exchange rates used for calculating the ECU's and EUA's equivalents

The central bank in each Member State communicates a representative market exchange rate for its currency against the United States dollar. The dollar has been chosen as giving the most representative rate in all financial centres. The rates are taken from the exchange markets at 2.30 p.m. They are communicated by the National Bank of Belgium to the Commission, which uses them to calculate an ECU/EUA equivalent first in dollars and then in the currencies of the Member States. If an exchange market is closed, the central banks agree on a representative exchange rate for the currency against the dollar which is communicated to the Commission.

Example: Calculation of equivalents for 1 December 1978

National currency amount of the ECU and EUA definition		1 December 1978 exchange rate against the USD	Equivalent in dollars of national currency	Equivalent in national currency of total USD amount
(a)		(b)	(c) (a) : (b)	(d) USD total × (b)
0.828	DM	1.9358	0.4277301	2.51689
1.15	FF	4.4495	0.2584560	5.78516
0.0885	UKL [1]	1.9364	0.1713714	0.671443
109	LIT	853.00	0.1277842	1 109.06
0.286	HFL	2.1035	0.1359638	2.73494
3.66	BFR	30.6675	0.1193445	39.8734
0.140	LFR	30.6675	0.0045650	39.8734
0.217	DKR	5.3885	0.0402709	7.00604
0.00759	IRL [1]	1.9364	0.0146972	0.671443

Total of dollar amounts   1.3001831

[1] The dollar exchange rate from London and Dublin is the number of dollars per currency unit rather than the number of currency units per dollar. Column (c) is therefore found for each of these two currencies by multiplying the value in column (a) by that in column (b); and column (d) by dividing the dollar equivalent of the ECU and EUA (c) by the rate in column (b).

The Commission also calculates an equivalent of the ECU and EUA for other currencies using for each its market rate against the dollar at 2.30 p.m.

3. Publication of the currency equivalents of the ECU and EUA

The daily equivalents in the different currencies calculated by the Commission are published correct to six significant figures in the 'C' edition of the *Official Journal of the European Communities*.

---

[12] This new communication annuls and replaces the previous communication (OJ C 225, 22.9.1978).
[13] From 28.12.1978.
[14] OJ L 379, 30.12.1978, p. 1.
[15] OJ L 356, 31.12.1977.

DOCUMENT 8 — Agreement between the central banks of the Member States of the European Economic Community laying down the operating procedures for the European Monetary System

The central banks of the Member States of the European Economic Community,

Having regard to the resolution of the European Council of 5 December 1978 on the establishment of the European Monetary System (EMS) and related matters;

Having regard to Regulation (EEC) No 907/73 of the Council of the European Communities of 3 April 1973 establishing a European Monetary Cooperation Fund;

Having regard to Regulation (EEC) No 3180/78 of the Council of the European Communities of 18 December 1978 changing the value of the unit of account used by the European Monetary Cooperation Fund;

Having regard to Regulation (EEC) No 3181/78 of the Council of the European Communities of 18 December 1978 concerning the European Monetary System;

Whereas the European Council has agreed to set up a scheme for the creation of closer monetary cooperation leading to a zone of monetary stability in Europe;

Whereas the said resolution provides that a European currency unit, the ECU, shall be at the centre of the European Monetary System and that the value and composition of the ECU shall, initially, be identical with the value and composition of the European unit of account (EUA);

Whereas under the terms of the said resolution:

(i) each currency will have an ECU-related central rate and the central rates will be used to establish a grid of bilateral parities or central rates;

(ii) fluctuation margins of 2.25% will be fixed around these bilateral central rates, although Member States not at present participating in the narrower margins mechanism may in the initial stage of the European Monetary System opt for wider margins of up to 6%, which must be progressively reduced as soon as economic conditions permit;

Whereas the said resolution further provides that a formula for an ECU-based basket shall be used as an indicator to detect divergences between Community currencies, and sets out the principles governing the operation of this indicator, which will be re-examined at the end of a period of six months;

Whereas this re-examination will also cover questions regarding imbalances accumulated by divergent creditor or debtor countries;

Whereas a Member State that does not initially participate in the exchange rate mechanism can do so at a later date and whereas it is therefore advisable to ensure cooperation between the central bank of such a State and the central banks of the participating States;

Whereas very short-term credit facilities of unlimited amount will be created;

Whereas the European Council has asked the central banks of the Member States of the Community to amend their Agreement of 10 April 1972 on the narrowing of the margins of fluctuation between the currencies of the Member States so as to embody the rules set forth in the said resolution;

Whereas in order to make provision for means of settlement the central banks have been asked initially to transfer to the European Monetary Cooperation Fund, in the form of revolving swaps against ECU, 20% of their gold holdings and 20% of their US dollar reserves, and thereafter to keep at least 20% of the said reserves on deposit with the European Monetary Cooperation Fund;

Have agreed as follows:

I. Exchange rate mechanism

Article 1 — Central rates in terms of the ECU

Each participating central bank shall notify the Secretariat of the Committee of Governors of the Central Banks of the Member States of the European Economic Community of a central rate in terms of the ECU for its currency. The Secretariat shall pass on this information to the other central banks and the European Communities.

Article 2 — Intervention rules

2.1 Each participating central bank shall notify the Secretariat of the Committee of Governors of the rates for compulsory intervention expressed in its currency, and the Secretariat shall pass on this information to the other central banks. These rates shall be fixed in relation to the bilateral central rates derived from the central rates in terms of the ECU referred to in Article 1 of the present Agreement. The market shall be notified of them.

2.2 Interventions shall in principle be effected in currencies of the participating central banks. These interventions shall be unlimited at the compulsory intervention rates. Other interventions in the foreign exchange market shall be conducted in accordance with the relevant guidelines that were adopted by the Committee of Governors in its Report of 9 December 1975 or that may be adopted in the future, or shall be subject to concertation among all the participating central banks.

Article 3 — Operation of the indicator of divergence

3.1 On either side of the central rate for its currency in terms of the ECU each participating central bank shall establish rates for its currency in terms of the ECU that will constitute 'thresholds of divergence'. These thresholds of divergence shall be calculated in such a way as to neutralize the influence of the differences in weights on the probability of their being reached; they shall be set at 75% of the maximum divergence spread, this being measured by the percentage difference between the daily rate and the central rate of a currency against the ECU when that currency is standing at the opposite pole from all the other currencies at the compulsory intervention rates referred to in Article 2.1 of the present Agreement. The necessary steps shall be taken to take account of the effects of the adoption of different maximum margins of fluctuation for the participating currencies and of the possible non-participation of a currency in the exchange rate mechanism.

3.2 If a currency crosses a divergence threshold, this shall entail the consequences set out in paragraph 3.6 of the Resolution of the European Council of 5 December 1978.

Article 4 — Method of calculating the values of the ECU in each currency

For the purposes of the operation of the indicator of divergence provided for under Article 3 of the present Agreement, the market value of the ECU in each currency shall be calculated by a uniform method as frequently as necessary and at least on the occasion of each daily concertation session among central banks.

Article 5 — Non-participation

Any central bank that is not participating in the exchange rate mechanism shall cooperate with the other central banks in the concertation and the other exchanges of information necessary for the proper functioning of the exchange rate mechanism.

II. Very short-term financing

Article 6 — Basic principles

6.1 To enable interventions to be made in Community currencies, the participating central banks shall open for each other very short-term credit facilities, unlimited in amount, in accordance with the conditions set out in Articles 7 to 16 of the present Agreement.

6.2 The financing operations concluded in this connection shall take the form of spot sales and purchases of Community currencies against the crediting or debiting of accounts denominated in ECU with the European Monetary Cooperation Fund (hereinafter referred to as 'EMCF').

Article 7 — Accounting procedures

7.1 The accounts opened for the central banks in the books of the EMCF shall be denominated in ECU. The conversion of currencies into ECU shall be effected at the daily rates for the ECU as established by the Commission's staff on the basis of the method adopted. The relevant rates shall be those ruling on the day on which the interventions were made.

7.2 The value date of the financing operations shall be identical with the value date of the interventions in the market.

Article 8 — Remuneration

8.1 The debtor and creditor interest rates applying to very short-term financing operations shall be the average of the official discount rates of all EEC central banks, weighted in accordance with their respective currencies' weights as derived from the ruling ECU central rates. This average shall be calculated once a month on the basis of the discount rates ruling on the last working day of the month and shall apply during the following month to all outstanding amounts in respect of very short-term financing operations.

8.2 Accrued interest shall be paid in ECU at each monthly settlement date or, between settlement dates, at the same time as advance liquidation of a debtor balance is effected.

Article 9 — Initial settlement date

The initial settlement date for a very short-term financing operation shall be the last working day preceding the sixteenth day of the second month following that in which the value date of the intervention fell.

Article 10 — Automatic renewal

At the request of the debtor central bank, the initial settlement date for a financing operation may be extended for a period of three months.

However:

(a) any initial settlement date many only be automatically extended once for a maximum of three months;

(b) recourse may only be had to the renewal facility referred to above if the relevant debt does not thereby remain continuously outstanding for more than six consecutive months;

(c) the total amount of indebtedness resulting from application of the present Article may at no time exceed a ceiling equal to the debtor quota of the central bank concerned under the short-term monetary support arrangement;

(d) if a central bank has recourse to the additional automatic borrowing facility for six consecutive months, the Committee of Governors shall take steps to ascertain whether the payments deficit of the country concerned is such that recourse to other means of financing, in particular short-term monetary support or medium-term financial assistance within the EEC, would be more appropriate.

Article 11 — Renewal by mutual agreement

11.1 Any debt exceeding the ceiling laid down in Article 10 (c) of this Agreement may be renewed once for three months subject to the agreement of the creditor or creditors in the EMCF.

11.2 Any debt already renewed automatically for three months may be renewed a second time for a further three months subject to the agreement of the creditor or creditors in the EMCF.

11.3 Debts and claims thus extended by mutual agreement shall be settled separately outside the provisions of Articles 12, 13 and 14 of this Agreement without prejudice, however, to the priority accorded to settlements carried out under those Articles. Offsetting or advance settlement of debts and claims of the kind for which provision is made in the present Article shall be subject to the agreement of all creditors and debtors in the EMCF, whatever their status.

Article 12 — Order of repayment of claims

12.1 Claims arising from financing operations carried out in accordance with Articles 9 and 10 above shall be settled on order of seniority; however, if a central bank's claim exceeds the amount of its creditor quota under the short-term monetary support arrangement, that central bank may request that the excess be treated for purposes of the next settlement as equal in seniority to the most senior claims of other creditor central banks.

12.2 All claims arising within the same monthly accounting period shall be regarded as of equal seniority. When a settlement covers a number of claims regarded as of equal seniority, each of the components of the settlement shall be distributed in proportion to the respective amounts of the claims.

12.3 The rules governing the order or distribution of settlements may be departed from subject to the agreement of all the parties to the financing operations carried out in accordance with Articles 9 and 19 of the present Agreement.

Article 13 — Automatic offsetting

13.1 All the debts and claims of a single central bank arising from the operations provided for under Articles 9 and 10 of the present Agreement shall, where appropriate, be automatically offset against each other.

13.2 Any new liability shall be offset against the most senior claim of the same central bank. Any new claim shall be offset against the most senior debt of the same central bank.

Article 14 — Advance repayment

14.1 Any debtor balance recorded in accordance with Articles 9 and 10 of the present Agreement may be settled in advance at the request of the debtor central bank:

(i) at any time in the currency of a creditor in the EMCF under Articles 9 and 10 of the present Agreement;

(ii) on the monthly settlement date by transfer of the means of settlement provided for in Article 16 of the present Agreement.

14.2 Any advance repayment shall be applied first to the most senior liabilities contracted under Article 10 of the present Agreement.

Article 15 — Working balances

The central banks may hold working balances in Community currencies within the limits laid down by the Committee of Governors. These limits may be exceeded only with the consent of the central bank concerned.

Article 16 — Means of settlement

16.1 When a financing operation falls due, settlement shall be carried out—in so far as it has not been settled in the first instance by means of holdings in the creditor's currency—entirely or in part by transferring ECU, with the proviso that a creditor central bank shall not be obliged to accept settlement by means of ECU of an amount more than 50% of its claim which is being settled. The balance shall be settled by transferring other reserve components in accordance with the composition of the debtor central bank's reserves as at the end of the month preceding the settlement.

These provisions shall be without prejudice to other forms of settlement agreed between creditor and debtor central banks.

Debtor balances in ECU settled by means of assets denominated in currencies and in SDRs shall be converted into such assets on the basis of the daily rates for the ECU established by the Commission's staff.

16.2 For the purposes of the preceding paragraph the composition of the debtor's reserves shall be determined on the basis of assets denominated in SDRs and in currencies. Nevertheless, gold holdings may also be taken into account if the price proposed by the debtor central bank is accepted by the creditor central bank. As far as assets denominated in SDRs and in currencies are concerned, the debtor central bank may choose which assets it will deliver in settlement.

16.3 If the debtor central bank no longer possesses ECU and wishes to acquire some, it shall apply in the first instance to central banks that are net accumulators of ECU or possibly to the EMCF. In the latter case, the ECU shall be acquired against the contribution of an equal percentage of the gold and dollar assets held by that central bank.

III. Creation, utilization and remuneration of ECU

Article 17 — Creation of ECU against contributions of gold and dollars

17.1 Each central bank participating in the exchange rate mechanism outlined in Chapter I of the present Agreement shall contribute to the EMCF 20% of its gold holdings and 20% of its gross dollar reserves as at the last working day of the month preceding the month in which the present Agreement takes effect; it shall be credited by the EMCF with an amount of ECU corresponding to these contributions.

Central banks that are not participating in the exchange rate mechanism referred to above may likewise make contributions in accordance with the terms of the preceding subparagraph.

17.2 The contributions referred to in Article 17.1 of the present Agreement shall be made available in the case of the participating central banks at the latest 10 working days after the implementation of the present Agreement or in the case of the non-participating central banks at the time of exercising the option referred to above.

17.3 The contributions of gold and dollars shall take the form of three-month revolving swaps against ECU which may be unwound at two working days' notice. These operations shall be concluded at flat rates.

17.4 For the purposes of the swap operations referred to in the present Article the value of the reserve components transferred to the EMCF shall be established as follows:

(i) for the gold portion, the average of the prices, converted into ECU, recorded daily at the two London fixings during the previous six calendar months, but not exceeding the average price of the two fixings on the penultimate working day of the period;

(ii) for the dollar portion, the market rate two working days prior to the value date.

17.5 Contracts shall be concluded between each central bank and the EMCF detailing the arrangements for the delivery of the gold and dollars to the EMCF and for their management in so far as this is entrusted to the central banks.

17.6 At the beginning of each quarter, when the swaps referred to in the present Article are renewed, the central banks and the EMCF shall make the necessary adjustments to these swaps, firstly to ensure that each central bank's contribution to the EMCF continues to represent at least 20% of its gold and dollar reserves on the basis of its gross reserve position recorded on the last working day of the preceding quarter and, secondly, to take account of any price or rate changes that may have occurred since the initial contribution or previous adjustment.

Article 18 — Utilization of ECU

18.1 ECU assets shall be used in intra-Community settlements within the limits and on the terms set out in Article 16 of the present Agreement.

18.2 The central banks may transfer ECU to one another against dollars, EEC currencies, Special Drawing Rights or gold.

18.3 For the purposes of meeting a decline in its dollar reserves a central bank may acquire dollars against ECU from the EMCF between two periodic adjustments, initially by unwinding a swap transaction.

18.4 The operations referred to in Articles 18.2 and 18.3 of the present Agreement shall not be carried out for the sole purpose of altering the composition of a central bank's reserves.

Article 19 — Remuneration

19.1 Central banks whose ECU assets are less than their forward sales of ECU shall pay interest to the EMCF on the difference between these two aggregates. The EMCF shall pay central banks whose ECU assets exceed their forward sales interest on the difference between these two aggregates. The amount of interest due shall be calculated in proportion to the average daily balances.

19.2 The rate of interest provided for in Article 19.1 of the present Agreement shall be determined in accordance with the provisions of Article 8 of the present Agreement. Such interest shall be paid monthly.

Article 20 — Liquidation

20.1 Save in the event of a unanimous decision to the contrary, the swaps of gold and dollars against ECU referred to in Article 17.3 of the present Agreement shall be unwound at the end of the two-year transitional period.

20.2 For this purpose central banks that are net users of ECU assets shall bring these back up to a level equal to that of their forward sales and central banks that are net accumulators shall transfer to the net users the excess of their ECU assets over their forward sales either directly or through the intermediary of the EMCF.

20.3 The transfers of ECU provided for in the preceding paragraph shall be effected in exchange for the currency of the central banks that are net accumulators, or in accordance with any other arrangements agreed between the parties, or against the transfer of reserve components in proportion to the composition of the reserves of the central bank repurchasing ECU, this composition being determined in accordance with the provisions of Article 16.2 of the present Agreement.

Article 21 — Institutional provisions

The Committee of Governors shall periodically review the operation of the present Agreement in the light of experience gained.

Article 22 — Termination of the Agreement of 10 April 1972

22.1 The present Agreement terminates and replaces, with effect from 13 March 1979, the Agreement of 10 April 1972, as amended by the Agreement of 8 July 1975, establishing a system for the narrowing of the margins of fluctuation between the currencies of the European Economic Community.

22.2 The present Agreement shall be drawn up in duly signed versions in English, French and German. A certified copy of the original in each language shall be sent to each central bank by the Secretariat of the Committee of Governors, which is required to retain the originals.

Done at Basle, 13 March 1979.

Banque Nationale de Belgique
C. de Strycker

Danmarks Nationalbank
Erik Hoffmeyer

Deutsche Bundesbank
Otmar Emminger   Karl Otto Pöhl

Banque de France
B. Clappier

Central Bank of Ireland
C. H. Murray

Banca d'Italia
Paolo Baffi

Nederlandsche Bank
J. Zijlstra

Bank of England
Gordon Richardson

DOCUMENT 9 — Instrument relating to short-term monetary support

The central banks of the Member States of the European Economic Community,

Having regard to the European Council's Resolution of 5 December 1978 concerning the establishment of the European Monetary System (EMS) and related matters,

Have agreed on the following provisions:

Article 1

The provisions of the Agreement of 9 February 1970 setting up a system of short-term monetary support, as amended by the Instrument of 8 January 1973 relating to the accession of the central banks of Denmark, Ireland and the United Kingdom and the Instruments relating to short-term monetary support dated 12 March 1974 and 13 December 1977 respectively, shall be amended as follows:

Article VI: *Technique of the operations*

The text of *paragraph 2* shall be replaced by the following text:

'If the facilities made available under the terms of this article are not utilized within one month they shall be cancelled. Utilization shall be for a period of three months and may be renewed twice for a period of three months at the request of the beneficiary central bank.'

The following sentence shall be inserted at the end of *paragraph 4:*

'They shall be denominated in ECU if the support is granted to a central bank in the form of a prolongation of a debt contracted by that central bank in the framework of the very short-term financing facilities, as defined by Article 6 of the Agreement of 13 March 1979 between the central banks of the Member States of the European Economic Community laying down the operating procedures for the European Monetary System.'

Article 2

The amounts of the debtor and creditor quotas assigned to each participating central bank in application of Article II.1 of the Agreement of 9 February 1970 as well as the total of the creditor rallonges and that of the debtor rallonges provided for under Article II.4 shall be established as from the date referred to in Article 4 of the present instrument by Annex 1 dated 13 March 1979, which shall cancel and replace all its precursors.

Article 3

Annex 1 dated 13 March 1979 referred to in Article 2 above is attached to the present instrument and forms an integral part of it.

Article 4

The present Instrument shall enter into force on the date on which the Agreement of 13 March 1979

between the central banks of the Member States of the European Economic Community laying down the operating procedures for the European Monetary System takes effect. It shall be drawn up duly signed in English, French and German. Annex 1 referred to above shall be duly initialled. One certified copy of the original in each language shall be sent to each central bank by the Secretariat of the Committee of Governors and of the Board of Governors of the European Monetary Cooperation Fund, which is required to retain the originals.

Done at Basle, 13 March 1979.

Banque Nationale de Belgique
C. de Strycker

Danmarks Nationalbank
Erik Hoffmeyer

Deutsche Bundesbank
Otmar Emminger   Karl Otto Pöhl

Banque de France
B. Clappier

Central Bank of Ireland
C. H. Murray

Banca d'Italia
Paolo Baffi

Nederlandsche Bank
J. Zijlstra

Bank of England
Gordon Richardson

ANNEX 1

13 March 1979

Quotas and rallonges in ECU [16]

1. *Quotas*

(a) *'Debtor quotas' and percentage distribution*

	in million ECU	per-centages
National Bank of Belgium	580	7.34
National Bank of Denmark	260	3.29
Deutsche Bundesbank	1 740	22.03
Bank of France	1 740	22.03
Central Bank of Ireland	100	1.27
Bank of Italy	1 160	14.67
Netherlands Bank	580	7.34
Bank of England	1 740	22.03
Total EEC	7 900	100.00

[16] The value of one ECU is defined by Regulation (EEC) No 3180/78 of the Council of the European Communities of 18 December 1978 changing the value of the unit of account used by the European Monetary Cooperation Fund.

(b) *'Creditor quotas' and percentage distribution*

	in million ECU	percentages
National Bank of Belgium	1 160	7.34
National Bank of Denmark	520	3.29
Deutsche Bundesbank	3 480	22.03
Bank of France	3 480	22.03
Central Bank of Ireland	200	1.27
Bank of Italy	2 320	14.67
Netherlands Bank	1 160	7.34
Bank of England	3 480	22.03
Total EEC	15 800	100.00

2. *Rallonges*

The total of creditor rallonges, and that of debtor rallonges, may not exceed 8 800 million ECU.

DOCUMENT 10 — Decision (No 12/79) of the Board of Governors of 13 March 1979

The Board of Governors of the European Monetary Cooperation Fund,

Having regard to the Resolution of the European Council of 5 December 1978 on the establishment of the European Monetary System (EMS) and related matters;

Having regard to Regulation (EEC) No 907/73 of the Council of the European Communities of 3 April 1973 establishing a European Monetary Cooperation Fund, and in particular Articles 3 and 4 thereof;

Having regard to Regulation (EEC) No 3180/78 of the Council of the European Communities of 18 December 1978 changing the value of the unit of account used by the European Monetary Cooperation Fund;

Having regard to Regulation (EEC) No 3181/78 of the Council of the European Communities of 18 December 1978 concerning the European Monetary System, and in particular Article 3 thereof;

Whereas the European Monetary Cooperation Fund is charged with arranging for the concertation necessary for the proper functioning of the exchange rate mechanism set up within the Community;

Whereas it is responsible for taking the necessary executive measures with a view to supplying the central banks with ECU against contributions of reserves,

Has decided as follows:

Chapter I: Exchange rate mechanism and very short-term financing

Article 1

The arrangements outlined in Chapters I and II of the Agreement of 13 March 1979 between the central banks of the Member States of the European Economic Community laying down the operating procedures for the European Monetary System (hereinafter referred to as the 'Agreement of 13 March 1979') shall be adopted by the European Monetary Cooperation Fund (hereinafter referred to as 'EMCF') to govern its administration of the very short-term financing facility.

Chapter II: ECU reserve assets

Article 2 — Creation of ECU against contributions of gold and dollars

2.1 The EMCF shall credit each bank participating in the exchange rate mechanism outlined in Chapter I of the Agreement of 13 March 1979 with an amount of ECU corresponding to the contribution of 20% of its gold holdings and 20% of its gross dollar reserves as at the last working day of the month preceding the month in which the present decision takes effect.

Central banks that are not participating in the exchange rate mechanism referred to above may likewise make contributions in accordance with the terms of the preceding subparagraph.

2.2 The contributions referred to in Article 2.1 above shall be made available in the case of the participating central banks at the latest 10 working days after the implementation of the present decision or in the case of the non-participating central banks at the time of exercising the option referred to above.

2.3 The contributions of gold and dollars shall take the form of three-month revolving swaps against ECU which may be unwound at two working days' notice. These operations shall be concluded at flat rates.

2.4 For the purposes of the swap operations referred to in the present article the value of the reserve components contributed to the EMCF shall be established as follows:

(i) for the gold portion, the average of the prices, converted into ECU, recorded daily at the two London fixings during the previous six calender months, but not exceeding the average price of the two fixings on the penultimate working day of the period;

(ii) for the dollar portion, the market rate two working days prior to the value date.

2.5 Contracts shall be concluded between the EMCF and each central bank detailing the arrangements for the delivery of the gold and dollars to the EMCF and for their management in so far as this is entrusted to the central banks.

2.6 At the beginning of each quarter, when the swap operations referred to in the present article are renewed, the EMCF and the central banks shall make the necessary adjustments to these swaps, firstly to ensure that each central bank's contribution to the EMCF continues to represent at least 20% of its gold and dollar reserves on the basis of its gross reserve position recorded on the last working day of the preceding quarter and, secondly, to take account of any price or rate changes that may have occurred since the initial contribution or previous adjustment.

Article 3 — Utilization of ECU

3.1 ECU shall be used in intra-Community settlements within the limits and on the terms set out in Article 16 of the Agreement of 13 March 1979.

3.2 The central banks may transfer ECU to one another against dollars, EEC currencies, Special Drawing Rights or gold.

3.3 For the purposes of meeting a decline in its dollar reserves a central bank may acquire dollars against ECU from the EMCF between two periodic adjustments, initially by unwinding a swap transaction.

3.4 The operations referred to in Articles 3.2 and 3.3 above shall not be carried out for the sole purpose of altering the composition of a central bank's reserves.

Article 4 — Intra-Community settlements

4.1 When a financing operation falls due, settlement shall be carried out—in so far as it has not been settled in the first instance by means of holdings in the creditor's currency—entirely or in part by transferring ECU, with the proviso that a credi-

tor central bank shall not be obliged to accept settlement by means of ECU of an amount more than 50% of its claim which is being settled. The balance shall be settled by transferring other reserve components in accordance with the composition of the debtor central bank's reserves at the end of the months preceding the settlement.

These provisions shall be without prejudice to other forms of settlement agreed between debtor and creditor central banks.

Debtor balances in ECU settled by means of assets denominated in currencies and in SDRs shall be converted into such assets on the basis of the daily rates for the ECU established by the Commission's staff.

4.2 For the purposes of Article 4.1 above, the composition of the debtor's reserves shall be determined on the basis of assets denominated in SDRs and in currencies. Nevertheless, gold holdings may also be taken into account if the price proposed by the debtor central bank is acceptable to the creditor central bank. As far as assets denominated in SDRs and in currencies are concerned, the debtor central bank may choose which assets it will deliver in settlement.

4.3 If the debtor central bank no longer possesses ECU and wishes to acquire some, it shall apply in the first instance to central banks that are net accumulators of ECU or possibly to the EMCF. In the latter case, the ECU shall be acquired against the contribution of an equal percentage of the gold and dollar assets held by that central bank.

Article 5 — Remuneration

5.1 Central banks whose holdings of ECU are less than their forward sales of ECU shall pay interest to the EMCF on the difference between these two aggregates. The EMCF shall pay central banks whose ECU assets exceed their forward sales interest on the difference between these two aggregates. The amount of interest due shall be calculated in proportion to the average daily balances.

5.2 The rate of the interest provided for in Article 5.1 above shall be determined in accordance with the provisions of Article 8 of the Agreement of 13 March 1979. Such interest shall be paid monthly.

Article 6 — Liquidation

6.1 Save in the event of a unanimous decision to the contrary, the swaps of gold and dollars against ECU referred to in Article 2.3 above shall be unwound at the end of the two-year transitional period.

6.2 For this purpose central banks that are net users of ECU shall bring these back up to a level equal to that of their forward sales and central banks that are net accumulators shall transfer to the net users the excess of their ECU assets over their forward sales either directly or through the intermediary of the EMCF.

6.3 The transfers of ECU provided for in Article 6.2 above shall be effected in exchange for the currency of the central banks that are net accumulators, or in accordance with any other arrangements agreed between the parties, or against the transfer of reserve components in proportion to the composition of the reserves of the central bank repurchasing ECU, that composition being determined in accordance with the provisions of Article 4.2 of the present decision.

Article 7 — Rescinding clause

This decision rescinds:

(i) Decision (No 2/73) of the Board of Governors of 28 June 1973 concerning settlements in gold;

(ii) Decision (No 6/75) of the Board of Governors of 8 July 1975 concerning the system for the narrowing of the margins of fluctuation between the currencies of the European Economic Community.

Article 8 — Entry into force

This decision shall enter into force with effect from 13 March 1979.

Done at Basle, 13 March 1979.

On behalf of the Board of Governors
The Chairman
C. de Strycker

DOCUMENT 11 — Decision (No 13/79) of the Board of Governors of 13 March 1979 modifying the short-term monetary support arrangement

The Board of Governors,

Having regard to the Council Regulation (EEC) No 907/73 of 3 April 1973 establishing a European Monetary Cooperation Fund, with particular reference to Article 3, third indent, and Article 4 thereof,

Has decided:

Article 1

The provisions contained in the instrument relating to short-term monetary support, concluded this day by the central banks of the Member States of the European Economic Community, are herewith adopted by the European Monetary Cooperation Fund as regulations governing its administration of the short-term monetary support arrangement.

Article 2

This decision shall apply as soon as the Instrument referred to in Article 1 above enters into effect; it shall be communicated to each central bank by the Secretariat of the Board of Governors of the Fund.

Done at Basle, 13 March 1979.

On behalf of the Board of Governors
The Chairman
C. de Strycker

DOCUMENT 12 — Council Regulation (EEC) No 2626/84 of 15 September 1984 amending Article 1 of Council Regulation (EEC) No 3180/78 changing the value of the unit of account used by the European Monetary Cooperation Fund

The Council of the European Communities,

Having regard to the Treaty establishing the European Economic Community,

Having regard to the Act concerning the conditions of accession of the Hellenic Republic and to the adjustments to the Treaties of 28 May 1979, [17] and in particular Annex VIII thereof,

Having regard to the proposal from the Commission,

Having regard to the opinion of the Monetary Committee,

_____

[17] OJ L 291, 19.11.1979, p. 17.

Having regard to the opinion of the Board of Governors of the European Monetary Cooperation Fund,

Whereas Article 1 of Council Regulation (EEC) No 3180/78 of 18 December 1978 [18] defines the ECU as the sum of amounts of currencies of the Member States;

Whereas Article 2.3 of the resolution of the European Council of 5 December 1978 on the establishment of the European Monetary System stipulates that the weights of the currencies in the ECU shall be re-examined and if necessary revised within six months of the entry into force of the system and thereafter every five years or, on request, if the weight of any currency has changed by 25%;

Whereas a re-examination has been carried out and the results indicate that a revision is appropriate;

Whereas in accordance with Article 2.3 of the resolution of the European Council of 5 December 1978, the revision should be made in line with underlying economic criteria and should not, by itself, modify the external value of the ECU;

Whereas Annex VIII of the Act annexed to the Treaty of Accession of the Hellenic Republic to the European Communities specifies that the drachma shall be included in the ECU before 31 December 1985 if, before that date, a revision of the ECU is undertaken;

Whereas the Greek authorities have taken the necessary measures to ensure that the inclusion of the drachma in the ECU will take place in conditions which ensure the smooth functioning of the ECU market,

Has adopted this Regulation:

Article 1

With effect from 17 September 1984 the composition of the ECU as laid down in Article 1 of Council Regulation (EEC) No 3180/78 of 18 December 1978 is amended as follows:

0.719	German mark,
0.0878	pound sterling,
1.31	French francs,
140	Italian lire,
0.256	Dutch guilder,
3.71	Belgian francs,
0.14	Luxembourg franc,
0.219	Danish krone,
0.00871	Irish pound.
1.15	Greek drachmas.

Article 2

This Regulation shall enter into force on 17 September 1984.

This Regulation shall be binding in its entirety and directly applicable in all Member States.

Done at Dromoland Castle, 15 September 1984.

For the Council
The President
A. Dukes

---

[18] OJ L 379, 30.12.1978, p. 1.

Versailles Summit, June 1982 — Statement of international monetary undertakings joined to the final declaration

Statement of international monetary undertakings

6 June 1982

1. We accept a joint responsibility to work for greater stability of the world monetary system. We recognize that this rests primarily on convergence of policies designed to achieve lower inflation, higher employment and renewed economic growth; and thus to maintain the internal and external values of our currencies. We are determined to discharge this obligation in close collaboration with all interested countries and monetary institutions.

2. We attach major importance to the role of the IMF as a monetary authority and we will give it our full support in its efforts to foster stability.

3. We are ready to strengthen our cooperation with the IMF in its work of surveillance; and to develop this on a multilateral basis taking into account particularly the currencies constituting the SDR.

4. We rule out the use of our exchange rates to gain unfair competitive advantages.

5. We are ready, if necessary, to use intervention in exchange markets to counter disorderly conditions, as provided for under Article IV of the IMF Articles of Agreement.

6. Those of us who are members of the EMS consider that these undertakings are complementary to the obligations of stability which they have already undertaken in that framework.

7. We are all convinced that greater monetary stability will assist freer flows of goods, services and capital. We are determined to see that greater monetary stability and freer flows of trade and capital reinforce one another in the interest of economic growth and employment.

European Parliament — Resolution of 16 February 1984

on the consolidation and completion of the European Monetary System within the framework of the proposals made by the Commission of the European Communities in March 1982

The European Parliament,

— having regard to the Communication from the Commission of the European Communities on the development of the European Monetary System EMS (COM(82) 133 final),
— having regard to the motions for resolutions on:

  — the creation of a European Savings Account in ECU in all the Community countries, [1]
  — the institution of an international competition to devise a symbol representing the ECU, [2]
  — the ECU, [3]
  — the creation of a fungible European currency, [4]

— having regard to the report of the Committee on Economic and Monetary Affairs (Doc. 1-1251/83),

A. Whereas around 50% of the external trade of the Ten takes place between Member States,

B. whereas it is of considerable importance that relations between the European currencies should be as stable as possible in that they reduce either the cost of exchange risk cover or the losses resulting from changes in the exchange rate,

C. whereas the aim of the EMS was to bring about a greater stability of exchanges rates between European currencies and not to reinstate a system of fixed and rigid parities,

D. whereas the EMS has been in operation now for almost five years and whereas this is a sufficient period on which to base a critical assessment of the functioning of the system,

1. Considers that the EMS has functioned relatively well to the extent that it has succeeded in bringing about a relative stabilization of the exchange rates between participating currencies and in effectively reducing their volatility, and also to the extent that the parity realignments have been carried out in an orderly manner as a result of joint deliberations and not of unilateral actions;

2. Observes, nevertheless, that the objectives of internal stabilization and convergence have not been attained to the extent expected, although the last two realignments did give rise to policy adjustments leading to improved convergence;

3. Points out that in the Member States which have experienced more rapid inflation, the fall in effective exchange rates has been more closely contained during the period of operation of the EMS than previously and, in contrast to the revaluation of the strong currencies, has been conducted in a more orderly manner;

4. Notes that while the system has withstood seven realignments and five years of serious disruption, it has also revealed weaknesses and inconsistencies which have held back its consolidation;

---

[1] Motion for a resolution tabled by Mr Israël (Doc. 1-425/83).
[2] Motion for a resolution tabled by Mr Sutra and others (Doc. 1-436/83).
[3] Motion for a resolution tabled by Mr Purvis (Doc. 1-748/82).
[4] Motion for a resolution tabled by Mr Israël (Doc. 1-1258/82).

5. Considers that the following have been particular weaknesses:
— the method of creating ECUs,
— the lack of coordination of exchange policies *vis-à-vis* third currencies,
— the fact that the ECU is not widely acceptable and negotiable and that it is non-exclusive and non-convertible,
— the lack of convergence towards internal stability;

6. Considers that the present circumstances warrant the re-opening of the debate on technical improvements to and the development of the EMS without delay; this is because
— the last two parity realignments have demonstrably led to pronounced shifts in economic policies towards closer convergence;
— most differences in inflation (except in the case of Greece, which is not a member of the European Monetary System) have been reduced;
— these results have been due to the constraint built in to the operation of the EMS.

Proposals for improving the EMS

A. *Improving the mechanisms*

7. Proposes that, in order to economize resources and limit interventions in dollars which upset relations between the currencies of the EMS, intervention within the margins by central banks in Community currencies should qualify for very short-term financing, which would be subject to a celing;

8. Considers it essential that, without waiting for the creation of the European Monetary Fund, the role of the EMCF should be reinforced and broadened by the establishment of a Standing Bureau of the EMCF which would operate under the authority of the Committee of Governors; this Bureau would gradually take over new responsibilities as and when a consensus is achieved on each within the Council of Ministers of Economic and Financial Affairs;

9. Considers that the first task to be entrusted to the Standing Bureau of the EMCF would be the effective and autonomous management of the various existing systems of very short-term financing, short-term monetary support and medium-term financial assistance; this would amount to transforming a network of bilateral relations into a multilateral system in which a Community institution could grant on its own behalf and under its responsibility a range of credit facilities which would vary in size and duration according to requirements;

10. Proposes moreover that the Standing Bureau of the EMCF should coordinate interventions in third currencies and, more particularly, policies *vis-à-vis* the dollar; to achieve this end, the bilateral swap agreements which exist between the Federal Reserve and the main European banks would have to be gradually replaced by a Fed-EMCF swap agreement which could both dampen the volatility of the dollar *vis-à-vis* the ECU and stabilize exchange rates within the EMS in so far as the currency used by the Federal Reserve to reimburse the EMCF would not necessarily have to be the same as the currency borrowed for the purposes of intervention;

11. Requests that the swap agreements which, under the present system, allow the creation of external EMS reserves and which can be unwound at two working days' notice, be consolidated and that transfers in dollars be made permanent, so that the EMCF may use them freely; this would enable the EMCF, at a later stage, to take over responsibility for the issuing of ECUs. These ECUs could be created initially against contributions of dollars, SDRs, national currencies or other reserve assets; later, they could be created against credits. At this stage, it would also be logical for debts and claims between participating central banks to be denominated and settled exclusively in ECUs. Initially, the acceptability level for the ECU in settling debts under very short-term financing between the central banks could be raised to 75%;

B. *Convergence*

12. Recalls that, under the existing EMS mechanisms, corrective interventions are obligatory or are triggered only when exchange rate stability is threatened, in other words when exchange rates reach the floor or the ceiling;

13. Proposes in this connection that a system of 'warning lights' such as wages costs, inflation differential, interest rates, budget deficits etc., be studied which, like the divergence indicator, would create a presumption of action by the Member States and an obligation for the Commission to make recommendations. Under such a system the appearance of a divergent trend in the economy of a particular country would become a subject of common concern which would have to be debated in the Council;

14. Calls on the Commission to make greater use of the power of recommendation conferred upon it by Article 11 of the Council Decision of 18 February 1974 [5] should one or more Member States depart from the guidelines laid down by the Council. Systematic and unjustified failure to observe these recommendations should be liable to be sanctioned by the suspension of certain Community credit facilities, such as the NCI or medium-term financial assistance or, at very least, the granting of such facilities ought to be made conditional upon compliance with the recommendations made by the Commission;

C. *The opening of the system*

15. Agrees with the Commission on the importance of promoting the international use of the ECU, which presupposes the rationalization of the procedures for creating ECUs and improvements to the return on and convertibility of the ECU;

16. Considers it important, in this connection, that approved third parties should be authorized to acquire existing ECUs freely from the participating central banks. The central banks could thereby mobilize their ECUs against dollars to settle their very short-term financing debts in ECUs without the total volume of ECUs in circulation being altered;

17. Is convinced furthermore of the need to authorize the EMCF, during a second stage, to create ECUs for approved third parties against contributions of reserve assets. Taking a broader and longer-term view, the EMCF could issue ECUs for third parties either against deposits of Community currencies or in the form of credits;

D. *Private use of the ECU*

18. Notes that the current rapid growth in the private use of the ECU corresponds to a real need, namely developing the use of a European currency as national economies become more integrated and as the number of intra-Community transactions increases;

19. Considers that the ECU offers unique advantages as a medium of exchange across national frontiers, with its complex composition based on member currencies broadly neutralizing particular fluctuations of individual currencies, so giving stability and continuity to the value of trading contracts and the return on investment decisions;

20. Considers that the national monetary authorities should not oppose this spontaneous trend of the markets, although they could monitor it more closely to ensure that it remains subject to the constraints of monetary stability and the general economic interest;

---

[5] OJ L 63, 5.3.1974.

21. Approves unreservedly the Commission's proposals concerning the use of the ECU and in particular:

— the recognition by all the Member States of the currency status of the ECU: the official quotation of the ECU on all the Community's exchange markets would be the culmination of such recognition;

— access by Community residents to transactions in ECU-denominated bonds under the general law;

— an ECU 'trade mark'. The EMCF should lay down general rules and ensure their implementation so as to avoid divergent practices which could harm the development of the ECU;

22. Considers nevertheless that it is necessary to go further and calls:

— on the Commission to put forward early proposals on the organization of a system of multilateral compensation for inter-bank transfers in ECUs and on the introduction of the official quotation of the ECU on all the exchange markets of the EEC;

— on the Member States to issue and circulate metal 1 ECU coins under the authority of the EMCF to popularize their use and to make Europeans more aware that they belong to a European monetary community;

— for the adoption of the symbol E (Greek epsilon) to represent the ECU;

— for concertation on the creation of a European savings account in ECUs in all the Community countries, as well as credit cards;

— on Member States to liberalize further their own domestic financial markets, by removing for example requirements that pension funds can invest only in domestically-issued equities, so that cross-frontier, private financial transactions can be promoted as a necessary prerequisite to the increased and effective use of the ECU and to legalize and encourage the use of the ECU as an accounting unit for company reports, etc.

23. Expresses its conviction that the development of the ECU is likely to contribute to a better balance in the development of international liquidity. This is because if the ECU were to become a real instrument of payment and a reserve asset it would offer an alternative to Euro-currencies;

24. Reiterates its request to the United Kingdom authorities for the pound sterling to join the exchange rate and intervention machinery of the EMS. In the event the objections and fears expressed in the United Kingdom have been shown to be exaggerated and the objections based on sterling's status as an oil currency and its inevitable volatility could be accommodated by allowing special fluctuation margins (6%) such as those applicable to the Italian lira.

One effect of such a move would be to help the European central banks to coordinate their exchange rate policy vis-à-vis the dollar by virtue of the special links which have always existed between those two currencies. It would also offer holders of reserve assets who wish to get out of dollars a European alternative other than the deutsch mark, which would alleviate the tension between the deutsch mark and the other European currencies;

25. Instructs its President to forward this resolution to the Council, the Commission and the Parliaments of the Member States of the Community.